Progress-Monitoring Assessments Primary

Intervention Station
A Reading Intervention Program

Harcourt School Publishers

www.harcourtschool.com

ISBN 10 0-15-372756-X

ISBN 13 978-0-15-372756-6

Table of Contents

Overview of the Phonological/ Phonemic Awareness Inventory

Phonological and phonemic awareness is an understanding that speech is composed of a series of sounds, or phonemes. Children who have difficulty attending to and manipulating the sounds in their language are likely to have problems learning to read. These children need additional oral language play to heighten their sensitivity to the phonemic basis of their speech.

The Phonological/Phonemic Awareness Inventory is a series of individually administered oral tests designed to assess a child's level of phonological and phonemic awareness. It assesses the important phonological and phonemic awareness skills of sound matching, sound isolation, sound blending, sound segmenting, sound deletion, and sound substitution. For reproducible inventories, see Copying Master pages 9 through 25. The Phonological/ Phonemic Awareness Inventory consists of the following tasks:

Contents of the Phonological/Phonemic Awareness Inventory

Task	Title of Task	Purpose of Task
1	Words in a Sentence	Assesses the child's ability to identify the number of words in a sentence.
2	Syllable Blending	Assesses the child's ability to blend individual syllables to produce a word.
3	Syllable Segmentation and Deletion	Assesses the child's ability to identify the number of syllables in a word; and delete a syllable to produce a new word.
4	Rhyming Words (Recognition and Production)	Assesses the child's ability to recognize words that rhyme; and produce a word that rhymes with another word.
5	Alliteration	Assesses the child's ability to indicate if two words do or do not begin with the same sound.
6	Onset/Rime Blending	Assesses the child's ability to blend word families to produce a word.
7	Phoneme Isolation (Initial)	Assesses the child's ability to listen to a word and isolate the beginning sound of that word.
8	Phoneme Isolation (Final)	Assesses the child's ability to listen to a word and isolate the ending sound of that word.
9	Phoneme Isolation (Medial)	Assesses the child's ability to listen to a word and isolate the middle sound of that word.
10	Phoneme Identity (Initial, Final, Medial)	Assesses the child's ability to identify the initial, final, or medial phoneme that is the same between words.
11	Phoneme Categorization (Initial, Final, Medial)	Assesses the child's ability to identify the word that has an initial, final, or medial phoneme that is different from other words.
12	Phoneme Blending	Assesses the child's ability to blend sounds together to say a word.

Task	Title of Task	Purpose of Task
13	Phoneme Segmentation	Assesses the child's ability to identify the individual sounds in a spoken word.
14	Phoneme Deletion	Assesses the child's ability to delete an individual phoneme in a word and orally produce the remaining part of the word.
15	Phoneme Substitution	Assesses the child's ability to substitute either the initial or final sound in a spoken word to produce a new word.

General Guidelines for Administering

The Phonological/Phonemic Awareness Inventory should be conducted individually in a quiet and comfortable setting. By administering the Inventory individually, the teacher can be sure the child is attending to the task and can gain insights into problems the child may be having.

You may use any one, or all, of the tasks. If you wish to obtain a comprehensive understanding of the child's phonological and phonemic awareness, administer all fifteen tasks. If you are interested in evaluating a specific aspect of phonological or phonemic awareness, administer only those tasks that are relevant to your needs. Whether you administer all fifteen tasks or just selected tasks, the tasks should be given in sequential order.

The Phonological/Phonemic Awareness Inventory covers a broad range of skills. Some of the skills such as identifying the number of words in a sentence (Task 1) can be performed by many beginning kindergarten children. Other skills, however, such as substituting initial and final sounds (Task 15) are not normally performed by children until the end of kindergarten or the beginning of Grade 1. Therefore, be cautious about asking students to perform tasks beyond their developmental level. **If a student misses four items in a row, discontinue testing of that particular task and move on to the next task. Also stop testing any time a student displays frustration and obvious discomfort with a task.**

There is no time limit. It will take approximately 30 minutes to administer all fifteen tasks. If possible, the tasks should be administered in a single session; however, they can be split up and given in two shorter sessions (e.g., two 15-minute sessions).

You and the child should be seated at a flat table or desk. The best seating location for you is facing the child, to facilitate clear diction and immediate recording of responses.

Become familiar with the directions and items. Specific directions for administering each task can be found on each Administering and Recording Form (see Copying Masters). The text after the word **"Say:"** is intended to be read aloud (directions to the teacher are *italicized*). The other information is for the teacher or examiner only and should not be read aloud. You should feel free to rephrase the directions, to repeat the samples, or to give additional examples to make sure the child understands what to do.

Before beginning the Inventory, spend a few minutes in light, friendly conversation with the child. Don't refer to the Inventory as a "test." Tell the child you would like to play some "word games."

Specific Directions for Administering

Follow these steps to administer the Phonological/Phonemic Awareness Inventory:

1. Duplicate a copy of the "Administering and Recording Form" for each task you will be administering and one "Summary of Performance" form. You will record a child's responses on the "Administering and Recording Form" and summarize the totals on the "Summary of Performance" form. The child will not need any materials.

2. Explain that the words the child hears and says every day are made up of sounds and that you will be saying some words and sounds and asking questions about them. Be sure to speak clearly.

3. Administer the tasks in sequential order. If the child has difficulty with the first four items or cannot answer them, stop giving that particular task and move on to another.

4. Follow the same basic procedures when administering each task. First, model the task so the child understands what to do. Second, administer the sample item and provide positive feedback to the child. Third, administer the items for that task. Fourth, record the child's responses for each item.

5. After giving the Inventory, record the child's scores on the "Summary of Performance" form. Use the "Performance Level" scale on the "Summary of Performance" form to determine the level that best describes the child's phonological and phonemic awareness. Children whose scores reflect minimal or emerging understanding may need additional oral language experiences. You may also wish to indicate specific observations from the Inventory, especially for those areas where the child had obvious difficulty with the task or required additional prompting.

Phonological/Phonemic Awareness Inventory

Summary of Performance

Name: _____

Task	Child's Score		
	Beginning of Year Date _____	**Middle of Year** Date _____	**End of Year** Date _____
Task 1: Words in a Sentence	/10	/10	/10
Task 2: Syllable Blending	/10	/10	/10
Task 3: Syllable Segmentation and Deletion	/10	/10	/10
Task 4: Rhyming Words (Recognition and Production)	/10	/10	/10
Task 5: Alliteration	/10	/10	/10
Task 6: Onset/Rime Blending	/10	/10	/10
Task 7: Phoneme Isolation (Initial)	/10	/10	/10
Task 8: Phoneme Isolation (Final)	/10	/10	/10
Task 9: Phoneme Isolation (Medial)	/10	/10	/10
Task 10: Phoneme Identity (Initial, Final, Medial)	/10	/10	/10
Task 11: Phoneme Categorization (Initial, Final, Medial)	/10	/10	/10
Task 12: Phoneme Blending	/10	/10	/10
Task 13: Phoneme Segmentation	/10	/10	/10
Task 14: Phoneme Deletion	/10	/10	/10
Task 15: Phoneme Substitution	/10	/10	/10
Total Score	**/150**	**/150**	**/150**

Performance Level: 0–50 Minimal Phonemic Awareness; 51–100 Emerging Phonemic Awareness; 101–150 Strong Phonemic Awareness

Phonological/Phonemic Awareness Inventory

Task 1: Words in a Sentence (Word Segmentation)

Administering and Recording Form

Task: The child will listen to a sentence and identify the number of words in the sentence.

Model: **Say:** I am going to say a sentence. I want you to repeat the sentence and clap to show me each word you hear in the sentence. Let's do one together. **I read a book.** *Repeat the sentence, clapping hands once for each word. Be sure to articulate each word separately.*

Sample: **Say:** Now you try one. After I say the sentence, you say it. Then clap to show me each word you hear in the sentence. **He hops down.** *Pause and wait for child to complete the task.* **Then say:** You're correct. You clapped your hands three times. *If child misses the task, demonstrate the correct answer.*

Say: Now listen to some more sentences. Repeat each sentence and clap your hands for each word you hear.

Name: _____

Item	Correct Response	Child's Response		
		Beginning of Year Date ____	Middle of Year Date ____	End of Year Date ____
1. Get out.	2			
2. She is sad.	3			
3. The fan is on.	4			
4. I like cats.	3			
5. They will have fun.	4			
6. Come here.	2			
7. You can do it.	4			
8. We sing.	2			
9. Go to bed.	3			
10. The frog hops.	3			

Total Score: _____/10

Comments: _____

Phonological/Phonemic Awareness Inventory

Task 2: Syllable Blending

Administering and Recording Form

Task: The child will listen to syllables and blend them together to say the word.

Model: Say: I am going to say some word parts. Then I want you to put them together to make a word. I will do the first one. Listen to these word parts: **tu–lip**. When I put the parts **tu–lip** together, they make the word **tulip**.

Sample: Say: Now you try one. Listen to these word parts: **pea–nut**. What word do you make when you put **pea–nut** together? *Pause and wait for child to complete the task*. **Then say:** You're correct. The word parts **pea–nut** make the word **peanut**.

Say: Now listen to some more word parts. You put the word parts together to make a word, and tell me the word.

Name: _____

Item	Correct Response	Child's Response		
		Beginning of Year Date ____	Middle of Year Date ____	End of Year Date ____
1. pop–corn	popcorn			
2. ham–mer	hammer			
3. lem–on	lemon			
4. sal–ad	salad			
5. side–walk	sidewalk			
6. play–pen	playpen			
7. tar–get	target			
8. tel–e–phone	telephone			
9. min–ute	minute			
10. back–pack	backpack			

Total Score: _____/10

Comments: _____

Phonological/Phonemic Awareness Inventory

Task 3: Syllable Segmentation and Deletion

Administering and Recording Form

Task: The child will listen to a word and identify the number of syllables.

Model: Say: I am going to say a word. I want you to repeat the word and clap to show the parts or syllables you hear. Let's do one together: **mitten**. *Repeat the word, clapping hands once for each syllable. Be sure to articulate each syllable clearly.*

Sample: Say: Now you try one. After I say the word, you say it. Then clap to show me each part or syllable you hear in the word: **toothbrush**. *Pause and wait for child to complete the task.* **Then say:** You're correct. You clapped your hands twice. *If child misses the task, demonstrate the correct answer.*

Say: Now listen to some more words. Repeat each word and clap your hands for each part or syllable you hear.

Name: _____

Item	Correct Response	Child's Response		
		Beginning of Year Date ____	Middle of Year Date ____	End of Year Date ____
1. kitchen	2			
2. key	1			
3. butterfly	3			
4. purse	1			
5. wagon	2			

Total Score: _____/5

Comments: _____

© Harcourt

Phonological/Phonemic Awareness Inventory

Task 3: Syllable Segmentation and Deletion (continued)

Task: The child will listen to a word and delete a syllable to create a new word.

Model: Say: Listen to this word: **flashlight**. If I take off the first word part, **flash**, the new word would be **light**.

Sample: Say: Now you try one. Listen to this word: **pancake**. If you take off the first word part, **pan**, what would the new word be? *Pause for response. Repeat the directions if necessary.* **Then say:** You're correct. The new word would be **cake**.

Say: Listen to some more words, take off the first word part in each word, and tell me what the new words would be.

Item	Correct Response	Child's Response		
		Beginning of Year Date ____	Middle of Year Date ____	End of Year Date ____
1. sunset (sun)	set			
2. anyway (any)	way			
3. uphill (up)	hill			
4. doghouse (dog)	house			
5. inside (in)	side			

Total Score: _____/5

Comments: _____

Phonological/Phonemic Awareness Inventory

Task 4: Rhyming Words (Recognition and Production)

Administering and Recording Form

Task: The child will listen to a word and then recognize a word that rhymes with it.

Model: Say: Let's play a word game. Listen to these two words: **bat — mat**. They are rhyming words because they end with the same sounds. Now you tell me, does **mop** rhyme with **top**? *Pause and wait for child to respond. If the child responds incorrectly, model a correct response.*

Sample: Say: Let's try another one. Does **rake** rhyme with **cane**? *Pause and wait for the child to respond.* **Rake** and **cane** do not rhyme. They do not end with the same sounds.

Say: Now listen to some more words. I will say two words and you tell me if they rhyme.

Name: _____

Item	Correct Response	Child's Response		
		Beginning of Year Date ____	Middle of Year Date ____	End of Year Date ____
1. cap, map	Yes			
2. dig, wig	Yes			
3. pet, mess	No			
4. cut, nut	Yes			
5. soap, note	No			

Total Score: _____/5

Comments: _____

Phonological/Phonemic Awareness Inventory

Task 4: Rhyming Words (Recognition and Production) (continued)

Task: The child will listen to a word and then produce a word that rhymes with it.

Model: Say: Let's play a word game. Listen to these two words: **sit — bit**. They are rhyming words because they end with the same sounds. Now you tell me a word that rhymes with **gate**. *Pause and wait for child to respond. Accept any word that rhymes with **gate** (e.g., date, late, plate). If the child cannot produce a rhyming word, model a correct response.*

Sample: Say: Let's try another one. Tell me a word that rhymes with **seal**. *Pause and wait for child to respond. Accept any response that rhymes with **seal** (e.g., deal, meal, real). If the child still cannot produce a rhyming word, discontinue this task.*

Say: Now listen to some more words. I will say a word and you tell me a rhyming word for the word that I say.

Name: _____

Item	Correct Response	Child's Response Beginning of Year Date ____	Middle of Year Date ____	End of Year Date ____
1. cap	Any word that rhymes with *cap*			
2. fun	Any word that rhymes with *fun*			
3. same	Any word that rhymes with *same*			
4. my	Any word that rhymes with *my*			
5. wet	Any word that rhymes with *wet*			

Total Score: _____/5

Comments: _____

Phonological/Phonemic Awareness Inventory

Task 5: Alliteration

Administering and Recording Form

Task: The child will listen to two words and will indicate if the two words do or do not begin with the same sound.

Model: Say: I am going to say two words. Listen carefully so you can tell me if the two words begin with the same sound: **pick, pail**. Listen again: **pick, pail**. The words begin with the same sound. **Pick** and **pail** begin with the same sound.

Sample: Say: Listen to these two words: **ladder, wagon**. Listen again: **ladder, wagon**. Do the two words begin with the same sound? (No) You're correct. **Ladder** and **wagon** do not begin with the same sound.

Say: Now listen to some more words. Tell me if the words begin with the same sound.

Name: _____

Item	Correct Response	Child's Response		
		Beginning of Year Date ____	Middle of Year Date ____	End of Year Date ____
1. may, cow	No			
2. table, pony	No			
3. chop, check	Yes			
4. father, fast	Yes			
5. bakery, banana	Yes			
6. sail, sauce	Yes			
7. jungle, yogurt	No			
8. daisy, dishes	Yes			
9. kitten, rabbit	No			
10. mask, month	Yes			

Total Score: _____/10

Comments: _____

Phonological/Phonemic Awareness Inventory

Task 6: Onset/Rime Blending

Administering and Recording Form

Task: The child will listen to word parts and will blend the sounds together to say the word.

Model: Say: I am going to say some word parts. Then I want you to put them together to make a word. I will do the first one. Listen to these word parts: **cl–ap**. When I put the parts **cl–ap** together, they make the word *clap*.

Sample: Say: Listen to these word parts: **l–ip**. What word do you make when you put **l–ip** together? **(lip)** You're correct. They make the word *lip*.

Say: Now listen again. I will say some word parts. You put them together to make a word, and tell me the word.

Name: _____

Item	Correct Response	Child's Response		
		Beginning of Year Date _____	**Middle of Year** Date _____	**End of Year** Date _____
1. sh–ip	ship			
2. b–ite	bite			
3. r–ake	rake			
4. pl–ant	plant			
5. f–all	fall			
6. r–ice	rice			
7. l–amp	lamp			
8. f–eet	feet			
9. c–ar	car			
10. b–ell	bell			

Total Score: _____/10

Comments: _____

Phonological/Phonemic Awareness Inventory

Task 7: Phoneme Isolation (Initial)

Administering and Recording Form

Task: The child will listen to a word and then will produce the initial phoneme in the word.

Model: Say: I am going to say a word. Then I am going to say just the beginning sound. Listen carefully for the beginning sound: **nose**. The beginning sound is **/n/**.

Sample: Say: Listen to another word. This time you tell me the beginning sound. Listen carefully: **hand**. What is the beginning sound in **hand**? (**/h/**) You're correct. **/h/** is the beginning sound in **hand**. *If the child tells you a letter name, remind the child to tell you the sound, not the letter.*

Say: Now listen to some more words. Tell me the beginning sound you hear in each word.

Name: _____

Item	Correct Response	Child's Response		
		Beginning of Year Date ____	Middle of Year Date ____	End of Year Date ____
1. name	/n/			
2. hip	/h/			
3. rain	/r/			
4. bunny	/b/			
5. farm	/f/			
6. gate	/g/			
7. door	/d/			
8. napkin	/n/			
9. seem	/s/			
10. tape	/t/			

Total Score: _____/10

Comments: _____

© Harcourt

Phonological/Phonemic Awareness Inventory

Task 8: Phoneme Isolation (Final)

Administering and Recording Form

Task: The child will listen to a word and then will produce the final phoneme in the word.

Model: Say: I am going to say a word. Then I am going to say just the ending sound. Listen carefully for the ending sound: **fin**. The ending sound is **/n/**.

Sample: Say: Listen to another word. This time you tell me the ending sound. Listen carefully: **hop**. What is the ending sound in **hop**? (**/p/**) You're correct. **/p/** is the ending sound in **hop**. *If the child tells you a letter name, remind the child to tell you the sound, not the letter.*

Say: Now listen to some more words. Tell me the ending sound you hear in each word.

Name: _____

Item	Correct Response	Child's Response		
		Beginning of Year Date ____	**Middle of Year** Date ____	**End of Year** Date ____
1. hut	/t/			
2. bug	/g/			
3. vine	/n/			
4. rib	/b/			
5. head	/d/			
6. like	/k/			
7. tap	/p/			
8. mail	/l/			
9. lime	/m/			
10. gas	/s/			

Total Score: _____/10

Comments: _____

Phonological/Phonemic Awareness Inventory

Task 9: Phoneme Isolation (Medial)

Administering and Recording Form

Task: The child will listen to a word and then will produce the medial phoneme in the word.

Model: Say: I am going to say a word. Then I am going to say just the middle sound. Listen carefully for the middle sound: **lap**. The middle sound is /a/.

Sample: Say: Listen to another word. This time you tell me the middle sound. Listen carefully: **sun**. What is the middle sound in **sun**? (/u/) You're correct. /u/ is the middle sound in **sun**. *If the child tells you a letter name, remind the child to tell you the sound, not the letter.*

Say: Now listen to some more words. Tell me the middle sound you hear in each word.

Name: _____

Item	Correct Response	Child's Response		
		Beginning of Year Date _____	**Middle of Year** Date _____	**End of Year** Date _____
1. hot	/o/			
2. rug	/u/			
3. bill	/i/			
4. hop	/o/			
5. fit	/i/			
6. pad	/a/			
7. deck	/e/			
8. pan	/a/			
9. cut	/u/			
10. let	/e/			

Total Score: _____/10

Comments: _____

Phonological/Phonemic Awareness Inventory

Task 10: Phoneme Identity (Initial, Final, Medial)

Administering and Recording Form

Task: The child will listen to three words and then identify the initial, final, or medial phoneme that is the same in all three words.

Model: **Say:** I am going to say three words. Listen carefully for a sound in each word that is the same: **ball**, **band**, **big**. The beginning sound in all three words is /**b**/. **Ball**, **band**, and **big** all begin with /**b**/.

Sample: **Say:** Listen to three more words. This time you tell me the sound that is the same in the words. Listen carefully: **win**, **hen**, **pan**. What sound is the same in **win**, **hen**, and **pan**? (/**n**/) You're correct. /**n**/ is the ending sound in **win**, **hen**, and **pan**.

Say: Let's do one more. Tell me the sound that is the same in the words. Listen carefully: **nap**, **cat**, **bag**. What sound is the same in **nap**, **cat**, **bag**? (/**a**/) You're correct. /**a**/ is the middle sound in **nap**, **cat**, and **bag**.

Say: Now listen to some more words. Tell me the sound that is the same in each group of words.

Name: _____

Item	Correct Response	Child's Response		
		Beginning of Year Date ____	Middle of Year Date ____	End of Year Date ____
Initial Phonemes				
1. sink, set, soap	/s/			
2. hill, have, heat	/h/			
3. milk, man, must	/m/			
Final Phonemes				
4. pig, dog, beg	/g/			
5. red, bad, code	/d/			
6. sat, net, lit	/t/			
Medial Phonemes				
7. men, wet, leg	/e/			
8. pond, log, hot	/o/			
9. cup, hut, run	/u/			
10. him, pit, dig	/i/			

Total Score: _____/10

Comments: _____

Phonological/Phonemic Awareness Inventory

Task 11: Phoneme Categorization (Initial, Final, Medial)

Administering and Recording Form

Task: The child will listen to three words and then identify the word that has an initial, final, or medial phoneme that is different from the other two.

Model: Say: I am going to say three words. Listen carefully to the beginning sound in each word: **rip, road, seat**. Which word has a different beginning sound than the other two: **rip, road, seat**? **(seat)** You're correct. **Seat** begins with a different sound than **rip** and **road**.

Sample: Say: Listen to three more words. This time you tell me the word that ends with a different sound than the other two. Listen carefully: **net, rob, mitt**. Which word has a different ending sound than the other two: **net, rob, mitt**? **(rob)** You're correct. **Rob** ends with a different sound than **net** and **mitt**.

Say: Listen to three more words. This time you tell me the word that has a different middle sound than the other two. Listen carefully: **wag, tip, hill**. Which word has a different middle sound than the other two: **wag, tip, hill**? **(/wag/)** You're correct. **Wag** has a different middle sound than **tip** and **hill**.

Say: Now listen to some more words. Tell me the word in each group that has a different beginning (ending or middle) sound.

Name: _____

Item	Correct Response	Child's Response Beginning of Year Date ____	Middle of Year Date ____	End of Year Date ____
Initial Phonemes				
1. cab, cup, mice	mice			
2. bean, heart, base	heart			
3. nest, jump, nail	jump			
Final Phonemes				
4. rake, bike, main	main			
5. fire, rope, beep	fire			
6. toad, hide, peel	peel			
Medial Phonemes				
7. pen, cob, get	cob			
8. nap, bag, cut	cut			
9. rock, well, not	well			
10. rub, nut, pig	pig			

Total Score: _____/10

Comments: _____

Phonological/Phonemic Awareness Inventory

Task 12: Phoneme Blending

Administering and Recording Form

Task: The child will listen to individual sounds and will blend the sounds together to say the word.

Model: **Say:** I am going to say some sounds. Then I want you to put them together to make a word. I will do the first one. Listen to these sounds: **/m/-/a/-/p/**. When I put the sounds **/m/-/a/-/p/** together, they make the word **map**.

Sample: **Say:** Listen to these sounds: **/n/-/o/-/t/**. What word do you make when you put **/n/-/o/-/t/** together? *Pause and wait for child to complete the task.* **Then say:** You're correct. The sounds **/n/-/o/-/t/** make the word **not**.

Say: Now listen again. I will say some sounds. You put the sounds together to make a word, and tell me the word.

Name: _____

Item	Correct Response	Child's Response		
		Beginning of Year Date ____	Middle of Year Date ____	End of Year Date ____
1. /p/-/e/-/t/	pet			
2. /l/-/a/-/n/-/d/	land			
3. /h/-/u/-/g/	hug			
4. /b/-/e/-/d/	bed			
5. /m/-/u/-/s/-/t/	must			
6. /d/-/o/-/t/	dot			
7. /k/-/u/-/p/	cup			
8. /d/-/i/-/g/	dig			
9. /r/-/a/-/m/-/p/	ramp			
10. /s/-/ee/	see			

Total Score: _____/10

Comments: _____

Phonological/Phonemic Awareness Inventory

Task 13: Phoneme Segmentation

Administering and Recording Form

Task: The child will listen to a word and then will produce each phoneme in the word separately.

Model: Say: I am going to say a word. Then I am going to say each sound in the word. Listen carefully for each sound. The word is **low**. The sounds in **low** are /l/-/ō/. *Be sure to articulate each sound separately. Do not simply stretch out the word.*

Sample: Say: Listen to this word. This time you tell me the sounds in the word. Listen carefully: **get**. What sounds do you hear in **get**? (/g/-/e/-/t/) You're correct. The sounds in the word **get** are /g/-/e/-/t/.

Say: Now listen to some more words. Tell me the sounds you hear in these words.

Name: _____

Item	Correct Response	Child's Response Beginning of Year Date ____	Middle of Year Date ____	End of Year Date ____
1. up	/u/-/p/			
2. hen	/h/-/e/-/n/			
3. man	/m/-/a/-/n/			
4. beep	/b/-/ē/-/p/			
5. road	/r/-/ō/-/d/			
6. it	/i/-/t/			
7. hike	/h/-/ī/-/k/			
8. jig	/j/-/i/-/g/			
9. bun	/b/-/u/-/n/			
10. face	/f/-/ā/-/s/			

Total Score: _____/10

Comments: _____

Phonological/Phonemic Awareness Inventory

Task 14: Phoneme Deletion

Administering and Recording Form

Task: The child will listen to a word and then delete a phoneme from the word to create a new word.

Model: Say: Listen to this word—**rice**. If I take off the /r/ sound, the new word would be **ice**.

Sample: Say: Now you try one. Listen to this word—**jam**. If you take off the /j/ sound, what would the new word be? *Pause for response. Repeat the process if necessary*. You're correct. The new word would be **am**.

Say: Listen to some more words and tell me what the new words would be.

Name: _____

Item	Correct Response	Child's Response		
		Beginning of Year Date ____	Middle of Year Date ____	End of Year Date ____
1. cold /k/	old			
2. race /r/	ace			
3. feel /f/	eel			
4. mat /m/	at			
5. win /w/	in			
6. neat /n/	eat			
7. rake /k/	ray			
8. beep /p/	bee			
9. nose /z/	no			
10. seed /d/	see			

Total Score: _____/10

Comments: _____

Phonological/Phonemic Awareness Inventory

Task 15: Phoneme Substitution

Administering and Recording Form

Task: The child will listen to a word and then replace either the initial or final phoneme to create a new word.

Model: Say: I am going to say a word. I want you to take off the first sound of the word and put in a new sound. Let's try one. If I change the first sound in **cap** to /l/, the new word is **lap**.

Sometimes I'll ask you to take off the end sound and put in a new sound. If I change the last sound in **wet** to /b/, the new word would be **web**.

Sample: Say: Change the first sound in **met** to /p/. What would the new word be? Yes, the new word would be **pet**.

Say: Now listen to some more words. Tell me the new words you would make.

Name: _____

Item	Correct Response	Child's Response		
		Beginning of Year Date ____	Middle of Year Date ____	End of Year Date ____
Initial Sounds				
1. lick /s/	sick			
2. mail /n/	nail			
3. tan /f/	fan			
4. dive /h/	hive			
5. net /v/	vet			
Final Sounds				
6. pig /t/	pit			
7. web /l/	well			
8. rode /b/	robe			
9. hat /m/	ham			
10. lime /k/	like			

Total Score: _____/10

Comments: _____

© Harcourt

Content of the Phonics Assessments

The content of these assessments parallels the instructional content of the Phonics Teacher Guide.

- Each Checkup is numbered sequentially. The lessons covered by a Checkup are indicated in parentheses.

- The Sound-Letter Relationships box tests some of the consonants, consonant blends and digraphs, and vowel patterns taught in the lesson covered. Beginning with Checkup 14, the sound-letter relationships are tested in the Decodable Words and Reading Sentences/Oral Reading sections.

- The High-Frequency Words box lists some of the high-frequency words that have been taught in each respective cluster of lessons.

- The Reading Sentences and Oral Reading passages contain both Decodable Words and High-Frequency Words taught in previous lessons.

- The Oral Reading passages may be used as Timed Reading Passages. Use the Oral Reading Fluency Recording Form on page 28 to record children's scores.

Administering the Assessments

The Checkups are informal assessments designed to inform instruction. They must be administered individually, since the items require oral responses. Two forms of each Checkup are provided in this manual—a form for the child to use, and a form for the teacher to use in recording responses. The student form is nonconsumable and can be reused for multiple administrations. A fresh copy of the teacher form should be created for each administration.

You should be able to administer a Checkup in about 5 minutes.

In general, follow these steps when administering the Checkups:

- Find a quiet setting in which to administer the Checkups. Seat the child on one side of a table or desk with you on the other side so you can record your responses unobtrusively. Explain to the child that you want to find out how well he or she understands the new sounds and words the class has been learning. Tell the child that you will write down his or her responses to help you remember what is said.

- Starting at the beginning of each Checkup, guide the child through each subtest. Give the child a reasonable amount of time to respond. Record the responses.

- On the Sound-Letter Relationships subtest, if the child gives an alternative sound for a vowel, ask the child if there is another sound that letter makes.

- If the child becomes frustrated and unable to respond, stop the assessment.

- If you are administering the Oral Reading section, have a stopwatch or a clock with a second hand available to time the child's reading.

- Wait to score and analyze the Checkup until after the child has left.

Scoring and Interpreting the Assessments

Scoring the assessments should be quick and straightforward. Each "item" is scored either correct or incorrect to obtain a child's raw score. The child's raw score is then compared to the expected score to determine whether to "Move Forward" or "Reteach."

Checkups 1 through 26

These checkups can consist of up to four sections or subtests. Follow these guidelines for scoring each subtest.

Sound-Letter Relationships

- Treat each letter or letter combination as an item.
- Place a checkmark over a letter or letter combination for correct responses.
- Record a child's response phonetically for any incorrect responses.
- Record the number correct in the space provided in the margin.

Decodable Words

- Treat each word as a separate item.
- Score the word correct if it is pronounced correctly.
- Score the word incorrect if it is pronounced incorrectly, and record the child's pronunciation phonetically.
- Record the number correct in the space provided in the margin.

High-Frequency Words

- Treat each word as a separate item.
- Score the word correct if it is pronounced correctly.
- Score the word incorrect if it is pronounced incorrectly, and record the child's pronunciation phonetically.
- Record the number correct in the space provided.

Reading Sentences

- Treat each word as a separate item.
- Record mispronunciations phonetically above the word.
- Circle any words that are skipped or omitted.
- Do not count repetitions and self-corrections as errors.
- Record the number of words read correctly in the space provided.

After scoring each of the four subtests and recording the scores in the margin, determine if the child meets the expected goal for each of the subtests. If the child meets the goal for 3 or 4 of the subtests, he or she is making adequate progress and should move forward in the program. If the child does not meet the expected goal for 2 or more of the subtests, he or she should receive additional practice and/or some reteaching of the decoding skills and high-frequency words tested before moving forward.

Oral Reading Accuracy and Fluency

- As the child reads the passage orally, record any mispronunciations and circle any omissions.
- Do not count repetitions and self-corrections as errors.
- Time the child as he or she reads. Make a single slash (/) in the text at the point the child reaches at 60 seconds.
- Treat each word as a separate item.
- Count the number of words read correctly and record that number in the space provided in the margin. Use the row numbers to help quickly count the number of words read correctly.

Oral Reading Fluency Recording Form

Name _____ Date _____

Oral Reading _____ Word Count: _____

FLUENCY SCORE

Total Words Read Per Minute _____

Number of Errors _____

Number of Words Read Correctly (WCPM) _____

✂ —

Oral Reading Fluency Recording Form

Name _____ Date _____

Oral Reading _____ Word Count: _____

FLUENCY SCORE

Total Words Read Per Minute _____

Number of Errors _____

Number of Words Read Correctly (WCPM) _____

Progress Chart Checkups 1–13

Name _____   Teacher _____

Checkup Number	Date Given	Sound-Letter Relationships	Decodable Words	High-Frequency Words	Reading Sentences	Action Taken		Comments
KEY: + = Met goal			— = Did not meet goal					
						Move Forward	Reteach	
1								
2								
3								
4								
5								
6								
7								
8								
9								
10								
11								
12								
13								

Progress Chart Checkups 14–16

Name _____ Teacher _____

| | | | | | KEY: + = Met goal | — = Did not meet goal | |
Checkup Number	Date Given	Decodable Words	High-Frequency Words	Reading Sentences	Action Taken		Comments
					Move Forward	Reteach	
14							
15							
16							

Progress Chart Checkups 17–26

Name _____ Teacher _____

| | | | | KEY: + = Met goal | | — = Did not meet goal | | |
Checkup Number	Date Given	Decodable Words	High-Frequency Words	Oral Reading		Action Taken		Comments
				Accuracy	Fluency	Move Forward	Reteach	
17								
18								
19								
20								
21								
22								
23								
24								
25								
26								

Checkup 1: (Lessons 1–10)

Letter Names   Goal: 4/5   Score ___/5

m	s	r	t	n

High-Frequency Words   Goal: 4/5   Score ___/5

I	a	my	a	I

☐ *Move Forward:* The child meets the goals for both subtests.

☐ *Reteach:* The child does not meet the goals for both of the subtests. Provide additional practice and retest.

Checkup 1

m	s	r	t	n

I	a	my	a	I

Checkup 2: (Lessons 11–20)

Sound-Letter Relationships   Goal: 4/5   Score ___/5

p	c	n	a	t

Decodable Words   Goal: 4/5   Score ___/5

nap	can	tan	ram	pan

High-Frequency Words   Goal: 4/5   Score ___/5

the	go	to	my	I

Reading Sentences   Goal: 12/14   Score ___/14

I can go.

Sam can nap.

My cat ran.

The ram ran to Pam.

☐ **Move Forward:** The child meets the goals for at least 3 of the 4 subtests.

☐ **Reteach:** The child does not meet the goals for 2 or more of the subtests. Provide additional practice and retest.

Checkup 2

p	c	n	a	t

nap	can	tan	ram	pan

the	go	to	my	I

I can go.

Sam can nap.

My cat ran.

The ram ran to Pam.

Checkup 3: (Lessons 21–30)

Sound-Letter Relationships   Goal: 4/5   Score ___/5

d	i	f	g	a

Decodable Words   Goal: 4/5   Score ___/5

dig	gap	fig	dip	fin

High-Frequency Words   Goal: 4/5   Score ___/5

like	he	come	go	to

Reading Sentences   Goal: 16/18   Score ___/18

Dan can dig.

I like to nap.

Come sit in the gap.

He can sit like a cat.

☐ **Move Forward:** The child meets the goals for at least 3 of the 4 subtests.

☐ **Reteach:** The child does not meet the goals for 2 or more of the subtests. Provide additional practice and retest.

Checkup 3

d	i	f	g	a

dig	gap	fig	dip	fin

like	he	come	go	to

Dan can dig.

I like to nap.

Come sit in the gap.

He can sit like a cat.

© Harcourt

Checkup 4: (Lessons 31–40)

Sound-Letter Relationships   Goal: 4/5   Score ___/5

> b   k   o   f   i

Decodable Words   Goal: 4/5   Score ___/5

> kit   bin   fog   bit   cob

High-Frequency Words   Goal: 4/5   Score ___/5

> here   this   me   where   do

Reading Sentences   Goal: 14/16   Score ___/16

> This dog bit me.
>
> Where do I sit?
>
> Here I come!
>
> Where did my kit go?

☐ **Move Forward:** The child meets the goals for at least 3 of the 4 subtests.

☐ **Reteach:** The child does not meet the goals for 2 or more of the subtests. Provide additional practice and retest.

Checkup 4

b   k   o   f   i

kit   bin   fog   bit   cob

here   this   me   where   do

This dog bit me.

Where do I sit?

Here I come!

Where did my kit go?

Checkup 5: (Lessons 41–50)

Sound-Letter Relationships   Goal: 4/5   Score ___/5

l	h	w	x	o

Decodable Words   Goal: 4/5   Score ___/5

hot	six	log	win	mix

High-Frequency Words   Goal: 4/5   Score ___/5

you	look	one	see	what

Reading Sentences   Goal: 18/20   Score ___/20

What box do you like?

I see one pot.

Can you look for the lid?

Did the wig fit him?

☐ **Move Forward:** The child meets the goals for at least 3 of the 4 subtests.

☐ **Reteach:** The child does not meet the goals for 2 or more of the subtests. Provide additional practice and retest.

© Harcourt

Checkup 5

| l | h | w | x | o |

| hot | six | log | win | mix |

| you | look | one | see | what |

What box do you like?

I see one pot.

Can you look for the lid?

Did the wig fit him?

Checkup 6: (Lessons 51–60)

Sound-Letter Relationships   Goal: 4/5   Score ___/5

v	j	y	z	l

Decodable Words   Goal: 4/5   Score ___/5

vet	zip	jog	led	yet

High-Frequency Words   Goal: 4/5   Score ___/5

we	want	they	who	are

Reading Sentences   Goal: 21/23   Score ___/23

We want to go in the jet.
They are not here yet.
We are in the red van.
She can zip it up.

☐ **Move Forward:** The child meets the goals for at least 3 of the 4 subtests.

☐ **Reteach:** The child does not meet the goals for 2 or more of the subtests. Provide additional practice and retest.

© Harcourt

Checkup 6

| v | j | y | z | l |

| vet | zip | jog | led | yet |

| we | want | they | who | are |

We want to go in the jet.

They are not here yet.

We are in the red van.

She can zip it up.

Checkup 7: (Lessons 61–70)

Sound-Letter Relationships   Goal: 5/6   Score ___/6

a	q	u	s	b	r

Decodable Words   Goal: 4/5   Score ___/5

quit	runs	bug	fun	bags

High-Frequency Words   Goal: 4/5   Score ___/5

and	give	have	let's	help

Reading Sentences   Goal: 29/32   Score ___/32

Dad and Pat give a little box to me.

Mom helps Ted get the big jugs down.

Let's quit now and sit in the sun.

I have one rug and two mats.

☐ **Move Forward:** The child meets the goals for at least 3 of the 4 subtests.

☐ **Reteach:** The child does not meet the goals for 2 or more of the subtests. Provide additional practice and retest.

© Harcourt

Checkup 7

a	q	u	s	b	r

quit	runs	bug	fun	bags

and	give	have	let's	help

Dad and Pat give a little box to me.

Mom helps Ted get the big jugs down.

Let's quit now and sit in the sun.

I have one rug and two mats.

© Harcourt

Checkup 8: (Lessons 71–80)

Sound-Letter Relationships   Goal: 5/6   Score ___/6

i   ck   a   p   t   n

Decodable Words   Goal: 4/5   Score ___/5

tap   lick   wink   hat   it's

High-Frequency Words   Goal: 4/5   Score ___/5

too   no   soon   late   hold

Reading Sentences   Goal: 29/32   Score ___/32

It's late, so come home soon.

Yes, you can help pick up the caps too.

Oh, she's not in the rink yet.

Rick and Pat hold the sick cat for the vet.

☐ **Move Forward:** The child meets the goals for at least 3 of the 4 subtests.

☐ **Reteach:** The child does not meet the goals for 2 or more of the subtests. Provide additional practice and retest.

© Harcourt

Checkup 8

i	ck	a	p	t	n

tap	lick	wink	hat	it's

too	no	soon	late	hold

It's late, so come home soon.

Yes, you can help pick up the caps too.

Oh, she's not in the rink yet.

Rick and Pat hold the sick cat for the vet.

Checkup 9: (Lessons 81–90)

Sound-Letter Relationships   Goal: 5/6   Score ___/6

| cl | th | o | sl | e | gl |

Decodable Words   Goal: 4/5   Score ___/5

| can't | call | rocking | then | sled |

High-Frequency Words   Goal: 4/5   Score ___/5

| thank | much | eat | how | said |

Reading Sentences   Goal: 27/30   Score ___/30

Isn't it time to make some good jam?

I am glad that I helped Glen find the sled.

Thank you for calling me first.

Who was looking for thin socks?

☐ **Move Forward:** The child meets the goals for at least 3 of the 4 subtests.

☐ **Reteach:** The child does not meet the goals for 2 or more of the subtests. Provide additional practice and retest.

© Harcourt

Checkup 9

cl   th   o   sl   e   gl

can't   call   rocking   then   sled

thank   much   eat   how   said

Isn't it time to make some good jam?

I am glad that I helped Glen find the sled.

Thank you for calling me first.

Who was looking for thin socks?

Checkup 10: (Lessons 91–100)

Sound-Letter Relationships   Goal: 5/6   Score ___/6

| ore | sl | u | br | or | sp |

Decodable Words   Goal: 4/5   Score ___/5

| sung | trap | she'll | store | brick |

High-Frequency Words   Goal: 4/5   Score ___/5

| water | food | live | says | feet |

Reading Sentences   Goal: 30/34   Score ___/34

Don't slip on your way to get in line.

I'll sing a song for you on the steps.

Go get some new drums at the store.

Every day she uses her backpack for school.

☐ **Move Forward:** The child meets the goals for at least 3 of the 4 subtests.

☐ **Reteach:** The child does not meet the goals for 2 or more of the subtests. Provide additional practice and retest.

© Harcourt

Checkup 10

| ore | sl | u | br | or | sp |

| sung | trap | she'll | store | brick |

| water | food | live | says | feet |

Don't slip on your way to get in line.

I'll sing a song for you on the steps.

Go get some new drums at the store.

Every day she uses her backpack for school.

© Harcourt

Checkup 11: (Lessons 101–110)

Sound-Letter Relationships Goal: 5/6 Score ___/6

sh	ch	qu	wh	ar	tch

Decodable Words Goal: 4/5 Score ___/5

chick	shut	star	when	quick

High-Frequency Words Goal: 4/5 Score ___/5

loud	gold	feel	under	grew

Reading Sentences Goal: 29/32 Score ___/32

Mrs. Match goes shopping every night.

My friends clapped when they saw me in the play.

Some fish were swimming under the ship.

The car could not go far in the rain.

☐ **Move Forward:** The child meets the goals for at least 3 of the 4 subtests.

☐ **Reteach:** The child does not meet the goals for 2 or more of the subtests. Provide additional practice and retest.

© Harcourt

Checkup 11

| sh | ch | qu | wh | ar | tch |

| chick | shut | star | when | quick |

| loud | gold | feel | under | grew |

Mrs. Match goes shopping every night.

My friends clapped when they saw me in the play.

Some fish were swimming under the ship.

The car could not go far in the rain.

© Harcourt

Checkup 12: (Lessons 111–120)

Sound-Letter Relationships   Goal: 5/6   Score ___/6

oa	er	ir	ow	ur	ar

Decodable Words   Goal: 4/5   Score ___/5

bird	goat	burn	row	fern

High-Frequency Words   Goal: 4/5   Score ___/5

money	always	other	work	join

Reading Sentences   Goal: 30/33   Score ___/33

The girl painted on her purple paper.

Can I please buy a nice fur coat?

Put a pretty bow on the smallest stack of books.

I am the tallest one in our family.

☐ **Move Forward:** The child meets the goals for at least 3 of the 4 subtests.

☐ **Reteach:** The child does not meet the goals for 2 or more of the subtests. Provide additional practice and retest.

© Harcourt

Checkup 12

oa   er   ir   ow   ur   ar

---

bird   goat   burn   row   fern

---

money   always   other   work   join

The girl painted on her purple paper.

Can I please buy a nice fur coat?

Put a pretty bow on the smallest stack of books.

I am the tallest one in our family.

Checkup 13: (Lessons 121–130)

Sound-Letter Relationships   Goal: 4/5   Score ___/5

| ee | ai | ea | ay | ow |

Decodable Words   Goal: 4/5   Score ___/5

| I've | rake | neat | we're | say |

High-Frequency Words   Goal: 4/5   Score ___/5

| hurry | dear | cool | four | move |

Reading Sentences   Goal: 24/27   Score ___/27

They're staying where it's warm and dry.

Keep your room neat and clean.

He baked a cake for Kate and Ray.

Where did Mother say to rake?

☐ **Move Forward:** The child meets the goals for at least 3 of the 4 subtests.

☐ **Reteach:** The child does not meet the goals for 2 or more of the subtests. Provide additional practice and retest.

Checkup 13

ee	ai	ea	ay	ow

I've	rake	neat	we're	say

hurry	dear	cool	four	move

They're staying where it's warm and dry.

Keep your room neat and clean.

He baked a cake for Kate and Ray.

Where did Mother say to rake?

Name _____ Date _____

Checkup 14: (Lessons 131–140)

Decodable Words   Goal: 4/5   Score ___/5

| nose | poke | bike | cent | gem |

Decodable Words   Goal: 4/5   Score ___/5

| mile | hedge | pose | joking | hiked |

High-Frequency Words   Goal: 4/5   Score ___/5

| pulled | walked | gone | because | hello |

Reading Sentences   Goal: 26/29   Score ___/29

Mike found four cents on the hike.

Rose wore a light brown badge.

I got tired riding my bike around the city.

Dad might like to see those gems.

☐ **Move Forward:** The child meets the goals for at least 3 of the 4 subtests.

☐ **Reteach:** The child does not meet the goals for 2 or more of the subtests. Provide additional practice and retest.

© Harcourt

Checkup 14

nose   poke   bike   cent   gem

mile   hedge   pose   joking   hiked

pulled   walked   gone   because   hello

Mike found four cents on the hike.

Rose wore a light brown badge.

I got tired riding my bike around the city.

Dad might like to see those gems.

Checkup 15: (Lessons 141–150)

Decodable Words   Goal: 5/6 Score ___/6

| cow | fight | loud | rude | cry | tie |

Decodable Words   Goal: 4/5 Score ___/5

| you'd | town | tube | lie | cloud |

High-Frequency Words   Goal: 4/5 Score ___/5

| only | table | earth | kinds | fooling |

Reading Sentences   Goal: 31/35 Score ___/35

We'd gone out to the store to get a pie.

The sky had cleared up by ten.

June heard the brown cow in the shed.

The tube of glue was high up out of reach.

☐ **Move Forward:** The child meets the goals for at least 3 of the 4 subtests.

☐ **Reteach:** The child does not meet the goals for 2 or more of the subtests. Provide additional practice and retest.

Checkup 15

cow   fight   loud   rude   cry   tie

you'd   town   tube   lie   cloud

only   table   earth   kinds   fooling

We'd gone out to the store to get a pie.

The sky had cleared up by ten.

June heard the brown cow in the shed.

The tube of glue was high up out of reach.

Checkup 16: (Lessons 151–161)

Decodable Words   Goal: 4/5   Score ___/5

kind	most	new	cool	hold

Decodable Words   Goal: 4/5   Score ___/5

candy	field	cold	mind	spool

High-Frequency Words   Goal: 4/5   Score ___/5

ready	nothing	toward	great	almost

Reading Sentences   Goal: 27/30   Score ___/30

The baby cried loudly most of the day.

The water in the new pool was very cold.

Drew told Tom the funniest stories.

I can't find my new blue stool.

☐ **Move Forward:** The child meets the goals for at least 3 of the 4 subtests.

☐ **Reteach:** The child does not meet the goals for 2 or more of the subtests. Provide additional practice and retest.

Checkup 16

kind   most   new   cool   hold

candy   field   cold   mind   spool

ready   nothing   toward   great   almost

The baby cried loudly most of the day.

The water in the new pool was very cold.

Drew told Tom the funniest stories.

I can't find my new blue stool.

Name _____ Date _____

Checkup 17: (Lessons 162–171)

Decodable Words   Goal: 5/6   Score ___/6

| fan | rip | net | mop | bud | cap |

Decodable Words   Goal: 5/6   Score ___/6

| beaches | fixes | trims | pencil | wagon | shops |

High-Frequency Words   Goal: 5/6   Score ___/6

| already | prove | sign | police | eight | sorry |

Oral Reading Have the child read the title and the entire passage. Start timing when the child begins reading.

Cats and Dogs	3
I like dogs. My friend, Pat, likes cats. I have a brown dog	16
named Ben. Pat has a black cat named Sam.	25
My dog runs and jumps. He fetches a big red ball.	36
Ben comes when I call him. Ben goes on long walks	47
with me. Ben is eight. I couldn't ask for a nicer pet.	59
Pat plays with Sam. Sam likes to chase a little red	70
ball. Sam likes people. When people pet Sam, she purrs.	80
At night, Sam sleeps on Pat's bed.	87
Dogs and cats make good pets. Which pet do you	97
like best?	99

Accuracy   Goal: 89/99   Score ___/99

© Harcourt

Checkup 17

fan	rip	net	mop	bud	cap

beaches	fixes	trims	pencil	wagon	shops

already	prove	sign	police	eight	sorry

Cats and Dogs

I like dogs. My friend, Pat, likes cats. I have a brown dog named Ben. Pat has a black cat named Sam.

My dog runs and jumps. He fetches a big red ball. Ben comes when I call him. Ben goes on long walks with me. Ben is eight. I couldn't ask for a nicer pet.

Pat plays with Sam. Sam likes to chase a little red ball. Sam likes people. When people pet Sam, she purrs. At night, Sam sleeps on Pat's bed.

Dogs and cats make good pets. Which pet do you like best?

Checkup 18: (Lessons 172–181)

Decodable Words   Goal: 5/6   Score ___/6

game	bike	green	pole	cube	team

Decodable Words   Goal: 5/6   Score ___/6

reached	seeing	raining	rowed	crane	flute

High-Frequency Words   Goal: 5/6   Score ___/6

guess	short	covered	ears	hundred	sugar

Oral Reading Have the child read the title and the entire passage. Start timing when the child begins reading.

My New Bicycle	3
I finally got a new bicycle. It is very special. It's green	15
and blue with red stripes. I ride my new bike through	26
our town. Riding is good exercise.	32
I like seeing everything when I ride around. Sometimes	41
I see children playing. Sometimes I see animals in the	51
woods. Sometimes I see people working at different jobs.	60
Tomorrow I'm going to ride my new bike to school.	70
It's a mile to my school. I just hope it doesn't rain.	82

Accuracy   Goal: 73/82   Score ___/82

© Harcourt

Checkup 18

| game | bike | green | pole | cube | team |

| reached | seeing | raining | rowed | crane | flute |

| guess | short | covered | ears | hundred | sugar |

My New Bicycle

I finally got a new bicycle. It is very special. It's green and blue with red stripes. I ride my new bike through our town. Riding is good exercise.

I like seeing everything when I ride around. Sometimes I see children playing. Sometimes I see animals in the woods. Sometimes I see people working at different jobs.

Tomorrow I'm going to ride my new bike to school. It's a mile to my school. I just hope it doesn't rain.

Name _____ Date _____

Checkup 19: (Lessons 182–191)

Decodable Words   Goal: 5/6   Score ___/6

| tight | mail | tray | dark | coat | row |

Decodable Words   Goal: 5/6   Score ___/6

| tie | purple | raincoat | baseball | raked | hoped |

High-Frequency Words   Goal: 5/6   Score ___/6

| coming | idea | laughed | curve | fair | clear |

Oral Reading Have the child read the title and the entire passage. Start timing when the child begins reading.

The Blue Jays	3
I am on a baseball team called the Blue Jays. My	14
brother is on the team, too. We like playing ball	24
together.	25
The Blue Jays play rain or shine. Our games	34
start at six. The coach likes to start on time. Fans	45
come to cheer us on.	50
In our last game, I caught a fly ball. It was hit	62
high, but right to me. I made the play of the night.	74
We ended up winning the game because of my catch.	84

Accuracy   Goal: 75/84   Score ___/84

© Harcourt

Checkup 19

| tight | mail | tray | dark | coat | row |

| tie | purple | raincoat | baseball | raked | hoped |

| coming | idea | laughed | curve | fair | clear |

The Blue Jays

I am on a baseball team called the Blue Jays. My brother is on the team, too. We like playing ball together.

The Blue Jays play rain or shine. Our games start at six. The coach likes to start on time. Fans come to cheer us on.

In our last game, I caught a fly ball. It was hit high, but right to me. I made the play of the night. We ended up winning the game because of my catch.

© Harcourt

Checkup 20: (Lessons 192–201)

Decodable Words   Goal: 5/6   Score ___/6

| money | ship | thank | bunny | city | path |

Decodable Words   Goal: 5/6   Score ___/6

| cried | dish | cent | dries | pillow | danger |

High-Frequency Words   Goal: 5/6   Score ___/6

| brought | early | question | popular | sure | enough |

Oral Reading Have the child read the title and the entire passage. Start timing when the child begins reading.

A Big Ship	3
Imagine a ship so big that it has a swimming pool.	14
Some ships can hold hundreds of people. They are	23
almost like floating cities. People can live on big,	32
expensive ships all year.	36
Just think, you could sail to all of your favorite	46
places. On board the ship, you could spend money	55
in the shops and enjoy some funny shows. You	64
could eat dinner on the top deck.	71
Believe it or not, you might miss standing on	80
the shore. You might be happy to get your feet	90
back on land.	93

Accuracy   Goal: 83/93 Score ___/93

☐ **Move Forward:** The child meets the goals for at least 3 of the 4 subtests.

☐ **Reteach:** The child does not meet the goals for 2 or more of the subtests. Provide additional practice and retest.

Checkup 20

money   ship   thank   bunny   city   path

cried   dish   cent   dries   pillow   danger

brought   early   question   popular   sure   enough

A Big Ship

Imagine a ship so big that it has a swimming pool. Some ships can hold hundreds of people. They are almost like floating cities. People can live on big, expensive ships all year.

Just think, you could sail to all of your favorite places. On board the ship, you could spend money in the shops and enjoy some funny shows. You could eat dinner on the top deck.

Believe it or not, you might miss standing on the shore. You might be happy to get your feet back on land.

Name _____ Date _____

Checkup 21: (Lessons 202–211)

© Harcourt

Decodable Words   Goal: 5/6   Score ___/6

> gem   girl   phone   write   nearly   kindness

Decodable Words   Goal: 5/6   Score ___/6

> judge   hopping   herd   know   heavy   laugh

High-Frequency Words   Goal: 5/6   Score ___/6

> woman   above   shoes   thumb   touch   sweat

Oral Reading Have the child read the title and the entire passage. Start timing when the child begins reading.

Photos for Fun	3
Josh likes taking photos for fun. He takes	11
pictures of everything he sees. There is no	19
stopping Josh when it comes to snapping	26
pictures.	27
Josh took a picture of a young woman	35
taking care of her father. Josh saw the	43
kindness in her eyes. A judge gave his photo	52
a first place prize.	56
Josh also took a picture of a little girl	65
he knew. She was skipping rope with her	73
cat. The photo made people laugh.	79

Accuracy   Goal: 71/79   Score ___/79

☐ **Move Forward:** The child meets the goals for at least 3 of the 4 subtests.

☐ **Reteach:** The child does not meet the goals for 2 or more of the subtests. Provide additional practice and retest.

Checkup 21

gem   girl   phone   write   nearly   kindness

judge   hopping   herd   know   heavy   laugh

woman   above   shoes   thumb   touch   sweat

Photos for Fun

Josh likes taking photos for fun. He takes pictures of everything he sees. There is no stopping Josh when it comes to snapping pictures.

Josh took a picture of a young woman taking care of her father. Josh saw the kindness in her eyes. A judge gave his photo a first place prize.

Josh also took a picture of a little girl he knew. She was skipping rope with her cat. The photo made people laugh.

© Harcourt

Checkup 22: (Lessons 212–221)

Decodable Words   Goal: 5/6 Score ___/6

| moon | boil | blue | deer | pout | paper |

Decodable Words   Goal: 5/6 Score ___/6

| robin | helpful | Jan. | suit | joy | harmless |

Decodable Words   Goal: 5/6 Score ___/6

| near | now | grew | reread | unhappy | misspell |

Oral Reading Have the child read the title and the entire passage. Start timing when the child begins reading.

Wonderful Soup	2
Dad and I enjoy cooking so we made some	11
wonderful soup. We bought everything we	17
needed for the soup at the store. Then we got	27
to work.	29
We read and reread the recipe. We didn't	37
want to make any mistakes. Dad said I was helpful	47
cutting up the foods.	51
When everything was in the pot, we added	59
seven cups of water. Then we boiled the soup	68
for an hour. Soon our family couldn't put their	77
spoons down.	79

Accuracy   Goal: 71/79 Score ___/79

☐ **Move Forward:** The child meets the goals for at least 3 of the 4 subtests.

☐ **Reteach:** The child does not meet the goals for 2 or more of the subtests. Provide additional practice and retest.

Phonics Checkup 22 73

Checkup 22

| moon | boil | blue | deer | pout | paper |

| robin | helpful | Jan. | suit | joy | harmless |

| near | now | grew | reread | unhappy | misspell |

Wonderful Soup

Dad and I enjoy cooking so we made some wonderful soup. We bought everything we needed for the soup at the store. Then we got to work.

We read and reread the recipe. We didn't want to make any mistakes. Dad said I was helpful cutting up the foods.

When everything was in the pot, we added seven cups of water. Then we boiled the soup for an hour. Soon our family couldn't put their spoons down.

Checkup 23: (Lessons 222–231)

Decodable Words   Goal: 5/6   Score ___/6

| prey   haul   care   wood   fought   preset |

Decodable Words   Goal: 5/6   Score ___/6

| chair   couldn't   taught   oversleep   dislike   loaves |

Decodable Words   Goal: 5/6   Score ___/6

| colder   sleigh   should   tallest   they'll   protection |

Oral Reading Have the child read the title and the entire passage. Start timing when the child begins reading.

Quite a Pair	3
Jen and Jan are quite a pair. They are best friends.	14
They like to laugh and have fun.	21
Jen is eight and so is Jan. Jen has long hair and	33
so does Jan. Jen and Jan weigh the same, but	43
Jen is taller than Jan.	48
Jen and Jan like the same things, too. The girls	58
like to read books and knit scarves. Jen and Jan	68
go to overnight camp and enjoy discovering	75
the coolest plants in the woods. Jen and Jan	84
share a cabin when they're at camp.	91

Accuracy   Goal: 81/91   Score ___/91

☐ **Move Forward:** The child meets the goals for at least 3 of the 4 subtests.

☐ **Reteach:** The child does not meet the goals for 2 or more of the subtests. Provide additional practice and retest.

© Harcourt

Checkup 23

prey   haul   care   wood   fought   preset

chair   couldn't   taught   oversleep   dislike   loaves

colder   sleigh   should   tallest   they'll   protection

Quite a Pair

Jen and Jan are quite a pair. They are best friends. They like to laugh and have fun.

Jen is eight and so is Jan. Jen has long hair and so does Jan. Jen and Jan weigh the same, but Jen is taller than Jan.

Jen and Jan like the same things, too. The girls like to read books and knit scarves. Jen and Jan go to overnight camp and enjoy discovering the coolest plants in the woods. Jen and Jan share a cabin when they're at camp.

Checkup 24: (Lessons 232–241)

Decodable Words   Goal: 5/6   Score ___/6

| quizzes | stretch | knives | sprout | sign | wrong |

Decodable Words   Goal: 5/6   Score ___/6

| tangle | pumpkin | simple | subtract | humble | complete |

Oral Reading Have the child read the title and the entire passage. Start timing when the child begins reading.

Wren's Garden	2
Wren decided to work in his garden. "You are good at digging," he	15
said to his two puppies. "You can be my partners."	25
He stretched strings from one end of the garden to the other. But	38
while Wren got sunflower and pumpkin seeds off the shelves, the puppies	50
tangled the strings.	53
"Stop it, Sprite! That's enough, Scrap!" Wren said. He carried the	64
puppies to another part of the garden in a hurry. "Dig here, please,"	77
he said.	79
Then he planted the seeds. "These need water to sprout," Wren	90
said. "I'll get the hose and sprinkler."	97
But when he came back, he saw the puppies were scratching up the	110
seeds.	111
"You are digging in the wrong place," Wren screamed. "I've had	122
enough, puppies," he said. "Let's go roughhouse under the spruce	132
instead."	133

Accuracy   Goal: 119/133   Score ___/133

☐ **Move Forward:** The child meets the goals for at least 2 of the 3 subtests.

☐ **Reteach:** The child does not meet the goals for 2 or more of the subtests. Provide additional practice and retest.

Checkup 24

quizzes	stretch	knives	sprout	sign	wrong

tangle	pumpkin	simple	subtract	humble	complete

Wren's Garden

Wren decided to work in his garden. "You are good at digging," he said to his two puppies. "You can be my partners."

He stretched strings from one end of the garden to the other. But while Wren got sunflower and pumpkin seeds off the shelves, the puppies tangled the strings.

"Stop it, Sprite! That's enough, Scrap!" Wren said. He carried the puppies to another part of the garden in a hurry. "Dig here, please," he said.

Then he planted the seeds. "These need water to sprout," Wren said. "I'll get the hose and sprinkler."

But when he came back, he saw the puppies were scratching up the seeds.

"You are digging in the wrong place," Wren screamed. "I've had enough, puppies," he said. "Let's go roughhouse under the spruce instead."

© Harcourt

Checkup 25: (Lessons 242–251)

Decodable Words   Goal: 5/6   Score ___/6

| recent | fudge | gentle | swarm | heard | taught |

Decodable Words   Goal: 5/6   Score ___/6

| solid | distrustful | flavor | rewrite | invisible | miscue |

Oral Reading Have the child read the title and the entire passage. Start timing when the child begins reading.

The Spelling Quiz

Sue was not the best speller in the world. Her teacher, Mr. Pearl,	3
	16
put a red circle around every misspelled word. Her papers were always	28
covered in red.	31
"I want to get one hundred percent on my next quiz," Sue told Mr.	45
Pearl.	46
"You will have to try harder," he said gently.	55
"I do try," Sue said, "but I don't know how to learn. The letters	69
swarm around on the page."	74
Mr. Pearl laughed. "This is what you do," he said. "I will give you	88
a preview of the test. Find the quietest room you can. Rewrite each word	102
ten times. If you make a mistake, turn the page over and redo the	116
exercise."	117
Sue did as he said. Happily, on her next quiz, she got one hundred	131
percent!	132

Accuracy   Goal: 118/132   Score ___/132

☐ **Move Forward:** The child meets the goals for at least 2 of the 3 subtests.

☐ **Reteach:** The child does not meet the goals for 2 or more of the subtests. Provide additional practice and retest.

© Harcourt

Checkup 25

recent   fudge   gentle   swarm   heard   taught

solid   distrustful   flavor   rewrite   invisible   miscue

The Spelling Quiz

Sue was not the best speller in the world. Her teacher, Mr. Pearl, put a red circle around every misspelled word. Her papers were always covered in red.

"I want to get one hundred percent on my next quiz," Sue told Mr. Pearl.

"You will have to try harder," he said gently.

"I do try," Sue said, "but I don't know how to learn. The letters swarm around on the page."

Mr. Pearl laughed. "This is what you do," he said. "I will give you a preview of the test. Find the quietest room you can. Rewrite each word ten times. If you make a mistake, turn the page over and redo the exercise."

Sue did as he said. Happily, on her next quiz, she got one hundred percent!

Checkup 26: (Lessons 252–257)

Decodable Words   Goal: 5/6 Score ___/6

canoe computer bisect decision nonfiction flexible

Decodable Words   Goal: 5/6 Score ___/6

beside   candle   create   reelect   under   float

Oral Reading Have the child read the title and the entire passage. Start timing when the child begins reading.

The Invention	2
Zoe's library books were overdue for the third time.	11
"How careless, Zoe!" cried Mrs. Columbo, the librarian. "You	20
have to be more responsible."	25
"I know," Zoe said. "I need to create a dependable invention that	37
will help me remember my library books."	44
She had one idea after another. "I could blast the books to the	57
library through a flexible hose," she said.	64
"That might be harmful to the books," Mrs. Columbo said.	74
"I could build a biplane out of bicycle parts and fly the books to	88
the library."	90
"That might be harmful to you," Mrs. Columbo said.	99
"What if I write a note and tape it to my backpack to remind me?"	114
Zoe asked.	116
"Now that's a sensible decision!" Mrs. Columbo said.	124

Accuracy   Goal: 111/124 Score ___/124

☐ **Move Forward:** The child meets the goals for at least 2 of the 3 subtests.

☐ **Reteach:** The child does not meet the goals for 2 or more of the subtests. Provide additional practice and retest.

Checkup 26

| canoe | computer | bisect | decision | nonfiction | flexible |

| beside | candle | create | reelect | under | float |

The Invention

Zoe's library books were overdue for the third time.

"How careless, Zoe!" cried Mrs. Columbo, the librarian. "You have to be more responsible."

"I know," Zoe said. "I need to create a dependable invention that will help me remember my library books."

She had one idea after another. "I could blast the books to the library through a flexible hose," she said.

"That might be harmful to the books," Mrs. Columbo said.

"I could build a biplane out of bicycle parts and fly the books to the library."

"That might be harmful to you," Mrs. Columbo said.

"What if I write a note and tape it to my backpack to remind me?" Zoe asked.

"Now that's a sensible decision!" Mrs. Columbo said.

Comprehension Contents

Name _____ Date _____

**Directions: Read the passage below. Fill in the circle in front of the best
answer to the question.**

Good Friends

Bob and Mike play after school. Bob likes to play with cars.
Mike likes to play with blocks. They take turns. First they play with
blocks. The boys make a town with blocks. Then Mike and Bob
play with cars. They drive the cars in the block town. Mike and
Bob are good friends. They take turns when they play.

1 Who are the characters in this story?

Ⓐ cars and blocks
Ⓑ Bob and his cars
Ⓒ Bob and Mike
Ⓓ Mike and his blocks

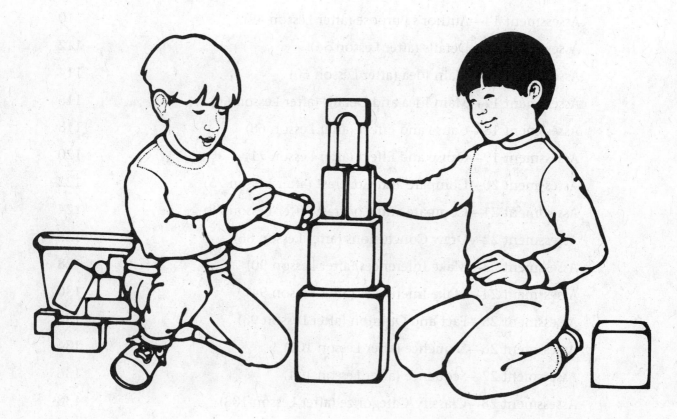

Comprehension Assessment: Assessment 1

© Harcourt

Name _____ Date _____

Directions: Read the passage below. Fill in the circle in front of the best answer to the question.

Run, Chip! Fly, Jay!

Chip is a chipmunk. Jay is a bird. Chip lives in a hole. Jay lives in a nest. Chip likes to eat seeds. Jay does too. They find a bird feeder. There are black seeds in the feeder. They eat seeds until they are full. Then, they see a cat. Run, Chip! Fly away, Jay! Chip and Jay are full and safe.

1 The two main characters in the story are

Ⓐ animals.

Ⓑ people.

Ⓒ cats.

Ⓓ birds.

Name _____ Date _____

Directions: Read the passage below. Fill in the circle in front of the best answer to the question.

Pet Show

Will and Kathy go to the pet show. There are cats, dogs, and rabbits. They see birds and fish too.

Will says, "I like this brown dog because he has a happy smile."

"Look at this bunny," says Kathy. "She has a pink nose."

Will and Kathy pet the cats. Then, the two friends watch the dogs do tricks. Will and Kathy see the rabbits hop and the rabbit ears flop.

Kathy says, "The pet show is fun. Let's come back next year."

1 Who are the main characters in this story?

Ⓐ Will and a brown dog

Ⓑ Kathy and Will

Ⓒ the rabbits

Ⓓ Kathy and the bunny

Comprehension Assessment: Assessment 2

© Harcourt

Directions: Read the passage below. Fill in the circle in front of the best answer to the question.

Tiger Purrs

It is time to go to sleep. Ann gets into her bed. She pulls the covers to her chin. Then her cat Tiger jumps on the bed. Ann rubs Tiger's chin, and then Tiger purrs. Ann rubs Tiger's ears, and then Tiger purrs some more. Ann pets Tiger's back, and then Tiger purrs and purrs. Finally, Ann gets too tired to pet Tiger. Ann closes her eyes. Tiger curls up beside Ann, and then Tiger purrs again.

1 Who are the characters in this story?

Ⓐ tigers
Ⓑ tigers and a girl
Ⓒ Ann and her bed
Ⓓ Ann and her Tiger

© Harcourt

**Directions: Read the passage below. Fill in the circle in front of the best
answer to each question.**

Early Bird

Robin is a happy bird. She lives in the park. In the morning,
Robin wakes early. She sings a song. Then she looks for food.
Robin flies to the pond. No food is there. She flies to the park
bench. No food is there. Then Robin flies to the green grass.
Today, Robin finds a worm to eat. The early bird gets the worm.
Robin likes living in the park.

Comprehension Assessment: Assessment 3

1 When does the story happen?

(A) late last night

(B) in the morning

(C) today at bedtime

(D) in the winter

2 Where does the story happen?

(F) at the zoo

(G) in a pond

(H) in a tree

(I) at the park

3 What is the story setting?

(A) an early summer morning at the park

(B) a winter night at the park

(C) a winter day at the zoo

(D) a summer day on a farm

Name _____ Date _____ **4**

Directions: Read the passage below. Fill in the circle in front of the best answer to each question.

Asleep at the Zoo

Yesterday, Jill went to the zoo. She saw the lazy bears. They were sleeping in a small cave. Jill saw the lions sleeping by a rock. Jill walked to the elephants. They were resting by a tree. "Why are the animals so tired?" asked Jill.

She walked to the large fish tank. She watched the fish swim. Small fish darted around in the water. Large fish glided smoothly. The turtles flapped their arms and legs. "At least the fish aren't sleeping!" laughed Jill.

Comprehension Assessment: Assessment 4

© Harcourt

1 When does the story happen?

Ⓐ today

Ⓑ late at night

Ⓒ last week

Ⓓ yesterday

2 Where does the story happen?

Ⓕ at the zoo

Ⓖ at school

Ⓗ in the ocean

Ⓘ in a jungle

3 What is the story setting?

Ⓐ today at the zoo

Ⓑ yesterday at the zoo

Ⓒ today at school

Ⓓ yesterday in the jungle

© Harcourt

Directions: Read the passage below. Fill in the circle in front of the best answer to each question.

Lazy Frog

Lazy Frog does not hop. He does not jump. He does not swim. Frog just sits on a log. He wants to be in the pond. But Frog is too lazy to move.

Turtle moves down the log. He is slow. Frog sees Turtle on the log.

"Where are you going?" asks Frog.

"I am going into the pond," says Turtle.

"I will come too," says Frog.

Lazy Frog gets on Turtle's back. Turtle moves down the log with Frog on top. Splash! They both go into the pond. What a lazy frog!

Comprehension Assessment: Assessment 5

1 What happens in the beginning of the story?

Ⓐ Turtle jumps in the pond.

Ⓑ Frog is lazy on the log.

Ⓒ Frog jumps in the pond.

Ⓓ Frog gets on Turtle's back.

2 What happens in the middle of the story?

Ⓕ Frog gets on Turtle's back.

Ⓖ Turtle jumps in the pond.

Ⓗ Frog and Turtle jump in the pond.

Ⓘ Turtle jumps on Frog's back.

3 What happens at the end of the story?

Ⓐ Turtle gets on Frog's back.

Ⓑ Frog jumps over Turtle.

Ⓒ Frog sleeps on the log.

Ⓓ Turtle and lazy Frog go into the water.

Directions: Read the passage below. Fill in the circle in front of the best answer to each question.

Pete and Penny Swim

Pete and Penny penguin want to learn to swim. They find the penguin teacher. She is by the water.

"Today we will learn to swim," says the teacher. "First, put your head down. Then, fall in the water. Next, flap your wings."

Pete puts his head down. Then he falls into the water. Pete flaps his wings. "I am swimming!"

"Now it is my turn," says Penny. She puts her head down. Splash! Penny dives in the water. She flaps her wings too. Pete and Penny swim all day in the cold water.

Comprehension Assessment: Assessment 6

1 What is the main event in the beginning of the story?

Ⓐ Pete jumps off the cold ice.

Ⓑ Penny jumps off the cold ice.

Ⓒ Pete and Penny find their teacher by the water.

Ⓓ Penny and Pete swim in the cold water.

2 What is the main event at the end of the story?

Ⓕ Pete and Penny swim in the water.

Ⓖ Pete finds the penguin teacher.

Ⓗ Penny finds the penguin teacher.

Ⓘ The teacher shows Pete and Penny how to swim.

3 What is the plot of the story?

Ⓐ Penny teaches Pete how to swim in the water.

Ⓑ Penny helps Pete find the teacher. Pete teaches Penny how to swim.

Ⓒ Penny and Pete are too cold to swim, so they walk on the ice.

Ⓓ A teacher helps Pete and Penny learn how to swim.

Directions: Read the passage below. Fill in the circle in front of the best answer to each question.

Book Report Trouble

Cassie felt very worried when she woke up. Today was her day to give a book report. Cassie was afraid to stand in front of the class.

That morning, Cassie's teacher spoke about manners. She explained that the class should sit quietly. They should be polite to the speakers in the front of the class.

When it was her turn, Cassie walked to the front of the class. At first, Cassie spoke softly, and her voice shook. She looked up and saw the kind smiles. Then she felt better, and she talked about her book. When her report was over, Cassie returned to her desk with a big smile.

© Harcourt

1 What is the problem in the beginning of the story?

Ⓐ Cassie speaks to the class, but they do not listen.

Ⓑ Cassie worries about giving her book report.

Ⓒ Cassie's teacher talks about manners.

Ⓓ Cassie forgets what her book is about.

2 What makes Cassie feel better during her report?

Ⓕ The students put their heads down.

Ⓖ Cassie remembers what the book is about.

Ⓗ Cassie sees the students smiling at her.

Ⓘ The teacher reminds the students to be polite.

3 What is the plot of the story?

Ⓐ Cassie is worried about speaking in front of the class. She feels better when the students smile politely.

Ⓑ Cassie forgets what her book is about.

Ⓒ Cassie's teacher talks about manners, but the students forget to smile.

Ⓓ When she stands in front of the class, Cassie forgets her story.

© Harcourt

Directions: Read the story title. Make a prediction. Fill in the circle in front of the best answer.

Jon Has a Shot

1 Read the title. What do you think the story is about?

Ⓐ Jon will drop a ball.

Ⓑ Mom has a shot in her arm.

Ⓒ Jon will play a game.

Ⓓ Jon will have a shot in his arm.

Directions: Read the first few sentences of the story. Make a prediction. Fill in the circle in front of the best answer.

Jon Has a Shot

Jon sat by his mom. He saw a sick girl. She had a red nose. Jon saw a sick boy. He had a bump on his leg.

2 Where do you think Jon is?

Ⓕ the store

Ⓖ the playground

Ⓗ the doctor's office

Ⓘ the beach

Comprehension Assessment: Assessment 8

Directions: Now read the whole story. Fill in the circle in front of the best answer.

Jon Has a Shot

Jon sat by his mom. He saw a sick girl. She had a red nose. Jon saw a sick boy. He had a bump on his leg.

"Jon, you can come in now," said a nurse. Jon and Mom went into a room. The nurse said, "Are you sick today?"

"No, Jon is not sick," said Mom. "Jon needs a shot. He will start school soon."

"Good. The shot will keep you well," said the nurse. Jon was brave. He got the shot in his arm.

3 Which prediction is correct?

Ⓐ Jon was sick.

Ⓑ Mom got a shot in her arm.

Ⓒ Jon played a game.

Ⓓ Jon had a shot in his arm.

© Harcourt

Name _____ Date _____

Directions: Read the passage below. Fill in the circle in front of the best answer to each question.

Lilly's Collection

Lilly's dad has many baseball cards. Lilly's friend has a collection of shells. Lilly wants to start a collection, too.

She looks in her room. Lilly wonders, "What do I want to collect?" She has a few marbles and some dolls. Then Lilly opens her scrapbook. On one page, she finds a yellow leaf from a tree in her yard. On another page, there is a red leaf from last fall. Lilly finds a third leaf that is very large. It is from an old, old tree in the playground. Lilly likes the leaves. Now Lilly knows what she will collect.

Comprehension Assessment: Assessment 9

1 What do you think Lilly will collect?

   (A) leaves

   (B) marbles

   (C) shells

   (D) baseball cards

2 What do you think Lilly will do next?

   (F) She will call her friend.

   (G) She will find more leaves.

   (H) She will buy baseball cards.

   (I) She will ask Dad for his collection.

3 How do the story details help you predict?

   (A) The author describes the shells.

   (B) The author describes the marbles.

   (C) The author describes leaves in a scrapbook.

   (D) The author describes Dad's cards.

Teacher Directions: Say: Look at the first two pictures. One picture shows
something that is real. One picture shows something that is
make-believe. Which picture is make-believe? Color in the circle
that is under the make-believe picture. Repeat for other items.

Comprehension Assessment: Assessment 10

© Harcourt

○   ○

○   ○

○   ○

Teacher Directions: Say: Look at the first two pictures. One picture shows something that is real. One picture shows something that is make-believe. Which picture is make-believe? Color in the circle that is under the make-believe picture. Repeat for other items.

Comprehension Assessment: Assessment 10   103

Name _____ Date _____

Directions: Read the passage below. Fill in the circle in front of the best answer to each question.

Bumble Bee

A bee is an insect. A bee's body has three parts. The bee has five eyes. Two eyes are large. Three eyes are small. A bee flies with four wings. A bee has six legs. A bee can sting you. Only female bees have stingers.

Bees fly from flower to flower. They collect pollen. This helps flowers grow. Bees can live in trees or in holes in the ground.

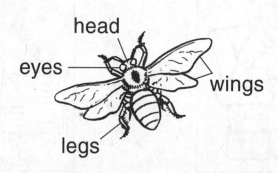

1 Is this selection fiction or nonfiction?

Ⓐ fiction

Ⓑ nonfiction

2 How do you know that this selection is fiction or nonfiction?

Ⓕ The selection is about bee facts.

Ⓖ The selection tells a story about a bee.

Ⓗ The story is make-believe.

Ⓘ The selection does not give information.

© Harcourt

Comprehension Assessment: Assessment 11

Name _____ Date _____ **11**

**Directions: Read the passage below. Fill in the circle in front of the best
answer to each question.**

Betty Bee Careful!

Betty is a bumble bee. She flies from flower to flower and
gathers pollen. Betty giggles when the pollen tickles her nose. She
buzzes to her hive inside a tree. There is sweet honey in the hive.
Betty's friends work in the hive, too. "Hi, Betty," buzz her friends
when she flies inside.

Just then, there is a roar. "I want honey!" yells a big black bear.
The bear wants to eat the honey from the hive.

"Be careful, Betty!" buzz her friends. "The bear might eat you,
too."

1 Is this selection fiction or nonfiction?

Ⓐ fiction

Ⓑ nonfiction

2 How do you know this selection is fiction or nonfiction?

Ⓕ The selection is about bee facts.

Ⓖ The selection tells a pretend story about a bee.

Ⓗ The story could really happen.

Ⓘ The selection explains a real event.

© Harcourt

Directions: Read the passage below. Fill in the circle in front of the best answer to each question.

I Am the New Boy

I walked down the long hall. There were new faces all around. I did not know one boy or girl. I pushed open the wooden door. I felt my face turn red. I did not want to cry. I had to be brave.

"Are you the new boy?" asked a kind man.

"Yes. I am Alex," I said softly.

The man smiled at me. He shook my hand. Then we walked to my new class.

1 What is the author's purpose?

Ⓐ to give you facts about schools

Ⓑ to give you directions to a school

Ⓒ to teach you a lesson about being mean

Ⓓ to tell a story

2 What is the author's point of view?

Ⓕ Alex is telling the story about himself.

Ⓖ A teacher is telling the story about a new boy.

Ⓗ The teacher is telling the story about himself.

Ⓘ Alex is telling the story about another person.

Directions: Read the passage below. Fill in the circle in front of the best answer to each question.

Bike Safety

When you ride a bike, you must be safe. You need to wear a bike helmet. It should be tight. It should not move on your head.

Check your bike. Is it safe to ride?

Follow rules when you ride your bike. Use hand signals. Tell people you are coming. Do not ride too fast. Ride in a line with other bikes. Slow down when others are around.

1 What is the author's purpose?

(A) to give directions about bike safety

(B) to tell a real story about a bike ride

(C) to entertain with a funny story

2 What is the author's point of view?

(F) A boy is telling a story.

(G) The author is giving information.

(H) The author is telling a story about someone else.

(I) A boy is telling a story about himself.

Directions: Read the passage below. Fill in the circle in front of the best answer to the question.

Banana Splits!

Jamie and her friends do cheers. They do cheers on the playground during recess. They are called the "Top Bananas." Jamie likes to do cheers with the "Top Bananas." They clap, jump, and chant fun cheers. After one cheer, Jamie does the splits. She stands on her legs. Then, one leg moves out. The other leg moves back. Jamie goes down slowly, and her legs stretch out. The "Top Bananas" clap and cheer for Jamie. Then Jamie hears a sound. *Rip.* Her pants split a little bit. *Rip!* Jamie's pants split a little more. *RIP!* Suddenly, there is a long hole in Jamie's pants. That's what you call a Banana Split!

1 What is the author's purpose?

Ⓐ to entertain with a funny story

Ⓑ to give directions on how to do the splits

Ⓒ to give information about bananas

Ⓓ to teach a lesson about being careful

© Harcourt

**Directions: Read the passage below. Fill in the circle in front of the best
answer to the question.**

The Two Baby Birds

Once upon a time, there were two baby birds: a lazy bird and a busy bird. They were resting in a meadow with Mother Bird. She was teaching her babies how to fly. The lazy baby bird said, "I am too tired to work. I will work later." The busy baby bird said, "I am tired too, but I will work *now*." The busy baby bird worked hard, and she learned to fly. She flew to their cozy nest in a tree.

Suddenly, a hungry fox tiptoed into the meadow. Mother Bird warned her lazy baby. "Fly! Fly! Or the fox will eat you!" Lazy baby bird flapped her wings, but she could not fly. Lazy baby bird jumped. But she still could not fly. Just then, the busy baby bird dropped a pinecone on the fox's head. The fox ran away as fast as he could. *Then* the lazy bird started to work.

1 What is the author's purpose?

Ⓐ to give facts about a fox

Ⓑ to give facts about baby birds

Ⓒ to tell a real story about a real bird

Ⓓ to teach a lesson about work

Name _____ Date _____

Directions: Read the passage below. Fill in the circle in front of the best answer to the question.

Bob Conners Is the Best!

VOTE
for
Bob Conners!

Bob is smart. Bob is funny.

Bob is good at sports.

You should vote for Bob Conners!

---

1 What is the author's purpose?

Ⓐ to give facts about sports

Ⓑ to teach a lesson about voting

Ⓒ to persuade people to vote for Bob

Ⓓ to entertain with a poem

Directions: Read the passage below. Fill in the circle in front of the best answer to the question.

A Very Big Change

A caterpillar is a busy creature. It eats leaves and grows a lot in the first stage of its life. It grows so big that it must shed its skin five different times. When the caterpillar sheds its skin for the last time, the new skin will turn into a thin shell of the chrysalis.

The chrysalis hangs under a sturdy stem. During that time, the caterpillar grows wings. After about 10 days, the butterfly emerges from the chrysalis. Its wings are wet and folded. The butterfly pumps fluid through its wings until they expand and dry. Soon the butterfly will fly away.

1 What is the author's purpose?

Ⓐ to tell a story about caterpillars

Ⓑ to entertain with a funny story about a butterfly

Ⓒ to inform about how a caterpillar becomes a butterfly

Ⓓ to teach a lesson about growing

Name _____ Date _____

Directions: Read the passage below. Fill in the circle in front of the best
answer to each question.

Stamp Book

Maria has a fun hobby. She saves stamps. Maria has one-hundred stamps! She gets her stamps from letters. Some stamps come from post cards. She has one old stamp. There is a wolf on the old stamp. The wolf has gray fur. The wolf has yellow eyes.

Maria keeps the stamps in a book. The book is full. She shows her book to friends. They like to count her stamps. Saving stamps is fun.

Comprehension Assessment: Assessment 15

1 How many stamps does Maria have?

(A) ten

(B) one hundred

(C) one

(D) fifty

2 What is on the old stamp?

(F) a wolf with gray fur

(G) a dog with yellow eyes

(H) a book

(I) a post card

3 Where does Maria get her stamps?

(A) from friends

(B) from books at the library

(C) from post cards and letters

(D) at the post office

Comprehension Assessment: Assessment 15

Directions: Read the passage below. Fill in the circle in front of the best answer to the question.

Tool Time

Some animals use tools. The tools help find food. Some animals use sticks. Some animals use rocks. An otter can use a rock. The otter hits with a rock. The rock breaks shells. Then the otter eats food in the shell. Animals are smart to use tools.

1 What is the main idea?

Ⓐ All animals use shells.

Ⓑ All animals use sticks.

Ⓒ Some animals use tools.

Ⓓ Otters eat food from shells.

© Harcourt

Directions: Read the passage below. Fill in the circle in front of the best answer to the question.

How Birds Move

Birds move in different ways. All birds have feathers. All birds have wings. Most birds can fly. But not all birds can fly. Penguins cannot fly. An ostrich cannot fly. Some birds swim. A penguin can swim very well. Ducks swim too. Some birds can run fast. An ostrich can run fast. Some birds like to walk. Some birds cannot walk at all! Birds move in many ways.

1 What is the main idea?

Ⓐ Birds move in different ways.

Ⓑ Feathers help birds fly.

Ⓒ Penguins swim.

Ⓓ Some birds run fast.

Directions: Read the passage below. Fill in the circle in front of the best
answer to each question.

Bright Feathers

Many male birds have colorful feathers. Male cardinals have
bright red feathers. The female cardinal is gray with pale red
wings. Another colorful male is the peacock. A male peacock has
shiny green-blue feathers. He can spread his feathers into a wide
fan. The tips of the feathers look like big blue eyes. The female
peacock is called a peahen. A peahen is brown. Like the female
cardinal, the peahen does not have colorful feathers. When you
see a very colorful bird, it is probably a male.

1 What is the main idea?

Ⓐ All birds have colorful feathers.

Ⓑ Most male birds have colorful feathers.

Ⓒ The peacock is pretty.

Ⓓ A peahen is brown.

2 What do peacock feathers look like?

Ⓕ the feather tips look like blue eyes

Ⓖ the feathers are bright red

Ⓗ the feathers are gray and pale red

Ⓘ the feathers are brown

3 How can you describe female cardinals?

Ⓐ They have bright red feathers.

Ⓑ They have blue wings.

Ⓒ They are gray with pale red wings.

Ⓓ They are more colorful than male cardinals.

© Harcourt

Directions: Read the passage below. Fill in the circle in front of the best answer to each question.

Baseball Language

Baseball has a special language. When you watch a game, you might hear the phrase "can-of-corn." This is a fly ball that can be caught easily. If your team is behind, it may be time for rally caps. A rally cap is a ball cap worn backwards or inside out. It is a way to cheer on your team. You're in trouble when you are in a rundown. A rundown is when a runner must dash back and forth between two bases. The player in a rundown does not want to hear the words "You're out!" The next time you watch a baseball game, listen for the special baseball language.

1 What is the main idea?

Ⓐ Rally caps are worn inside out.

Ⓑ Baseball has a special language.

Ⓒ There are rundowns during games.

Ⓓ A can-of-corn is a fly ball.

2 Why do people wear rally caps?

Ⓕ to cheer on their team

Ⓖ to keep warm

Ⓗ when it starts to rain

Ⓘ when a player is in a rundown

3 What does a player in a rundown do?

Ⓐ stops running

Ⓑ catches a fly ball

Ⓒ tries to hear the words "You're out!"

Ⓓ runs back and forth between bases

Directions: Read the passage below. Fill in the circle in front of the best answer to each question.

Bump, Bump, Crash

"Who has the ball?" the kids asked.

"I have it," said Dan. Then he ran into his house. Dan ran up the steps. He ran down the hall. He ran to his room. Dan got the ball.

"Here I come!" called Dan to his friends. He ran down the hall. Then he stopped. He put the ball down by the steps. Dan ran back to his room. Just then, the ball rolled. It rolled down the steps. Bump, bump, bump. It hit each step. Then, *crash*! The ball hit Mom's vase. Dan felt very bad.

© Harcourt

1 Dan runs in his house to

Ⓐ hide the vase.

Ⓑ find his friends.

Ⓒ find the ball.

Ⓓ hide from Mom.

2 What happens when Dan puts the ball down?

Ⓕ He forgets the ball.

Ⓖ The friends go home.

Ⓗ Mom kicks the ball.

Ⓘ The ball rolls down the steps.

3 What causes the vase to break?

Ⓐ Dan's ball hits the vase.

Ⓑ Dan hits the vase.

Ⓒ Mom drops the vase.

Ⓓ The vase falls down the steps.

Comprehension Assessment: Assessment 18

Directions: Read the passage below. Fill in the circle in front of the best answer to each question.

Sticky Fingers

Jennifer's school will celebrate Valentine's Day soon. Jennifer is making valentines for her class. She cuts white paper into heart shapes. She writes "I Like You" on the paper hearts. Jennifer colors the hearts pink and red. She glues on white lace and fancy ribbon.

The glue makes Jennifer's fingers feel sticky. Little bits of paper are sticking to Jennifer's fingers because of the glue. After making five valentines, bits of ribbon and lace are hanging from Jennifer's fingers too.

Soon Jennifer's fingers are so messy she must stop her project and wash her hands.

1 What causes bits of paper to stick to Jennifer's fingers?

   Ⓐ glue

   Ⓑ a magnet

   Ⓒ tape

   Ⓓ sticky juice

2 Jennifer stops her project because

   Ⓕ her mom calls her.

   Ⓖ her friends come in.

   Ⓗ she needs to wash her hands.

   Ⓘ it is Valentine's Day.

3 Why is Jennifer making valentines?

   Ⓐ She forgot to make one for her mother.

   Ⓑ She likes hearts.

   Ⓒ Her school will celebrate Valentine's Day soon.

   Ⓓ She likes to work with paper and glue.

Name _____ Date _____

**Directions: Read the passage below. Fill in the circle in front of the best
answer to each question.**

Apples and Pears

Fruit is good for you. We need to eat fruit. Apples are fruit.
Pears are fruit. Apples grow on trees. Pears grow on trees, too.
Both apples and pears have seeds.

Apples can be red. Apples can be yellow and green. Pears are
not red. Most pears are yellow or green. Apples are crisp. They
crunch when you bite them. Most pears are soft. Apples are
round. Pears look like light bulbs.

Apples and pears are good to eat.

Comprehension Assessment: Assessment 20

1 How are pears and apples alike?

Ⓐ Both are round like balls.

Ⓑ Both grow on trees.

Ⓒ Both are soft.

Ⓓ Both are red.

2 How are pears and apples different?

Ⓕ A pear has seeds. An apple does not have seeds.

Ⓖ Pears are soft. Apples are crisp.

Ⓗ Pears grow on trees. Apples grow on vines.

Ⓘ An apple is a fruit. A pear is not a fruit.

3 How can we compare apples and pears?

Ⓐ Both are fruit.

Ⓑ Both are red.

Ⓒ Both are round.

Ⓓ Both are soft.

Directions: Read the passage below. Fill in the circle in front of the best answer to each question.

Birthday Pie?

Today is Jason's birthday, and he is having a birthday party. Five friends will come to his house after school. They will eat lots of pizza. The boys will tell jokes and play games. Jason will open a few gifts. Then they will eat dessert. Will they eat birthday cake? No! Jason doesn't like to eat cake on his birthday. He thinks the fluffy frosting is too sweet, and he does not like the soft, spongy cake.

Jason likes pie better than cake. Pie has a crust at the bottom of the pie pan. The crust is dry and crumbly. He likes cherry pie the best. The fruit tastes tart and tangy. Cherry pie does not taste as sweet as cake. Jason thinks that pie is a perfect dessert for a birthday party.

Mom will stick the candles on top. Then it will be time to sing "Happy Birthday to You"!

Comprehension Assessment: Assessment 21

1 How is a pie like a cake?

Ⓐ both are desserts
Ⓑ both have a crust
Ⓒ both have frosting
Ⓓ both are tart

2 How are pies and cakes different?

Ⓕ A pie has frosting. A cake has crust.
Ⓖ A pie is soft and spongy. A cake is not soft and spongy.
Ⓗ A pie has crust. A cake has frosting.
Ⓘ A pie is dessert. Cake is not a dessert.

3 Which of the following statements does <u>not</u> contrast pie and cake?

Ⓐ Cake is sweet. Cherry pie is tart.
Ⓑ Both are desserts. Both are sweet.
Ⓒ Cake has frosting. Pie does not have frosting.
Ⓓ Pie has a crust. Cake does not have crust.

© Harcourt

**Directions: Read the passage below. Fill in the circle in front of the best
answer to each question.**

Tim's Tired Time

Mom put a box of tissues on the table. She felt Tim's head. His
head felt too warm. "Stay in bed today," said Mom. "No school for
you." Tim's nose was red. He sneezed a lot. Tim felt sleepy, so he
took a nap.

Mom fed Tim hot chicken soup. It tasted salty and warm. The
soup made Tim feel better. He read a book in bed. Then, he took
another nap. He slept a long time.

Mom gave Tim a cup of juice. He snacked on crackers. He
colored a picture, and he listened to music. He sneezed a few
times. Tim felt tired again so he closed his eyes.

When Tim woke up, he had more soup. His nose was not as red.
Mom felt his head. "You can go to school tomorrow."

1 Why does Mom put tissues on the table?

Ⓐ She likes the pretty box.

Ⓑ Tim has a cold.

Ⓒ She is crying.

Ⓓ Tim is crying.

2 Why does Tim take so many naps?

Ⓕ He likes to sleep.

Ⓖ He stayed up late the night before.

Ⓗ He is sick.

Ⓘ He is on a vacation.

3 Mom will let Tim go back to school because

Ⓐ he finished his soup.

Ⓑ his head feels too warm.

Ⓒ it is Monday.

Ⓓ he is better now.

© Harcourt

Directions: Read the passage below. Fill in the circle in front of the best answer to each question.

Pumpkins

The big green tractor rumbled down the road. The tractor stopped, and Molly got on the wagon. The tractor pulled the wagon down a dirt road. The wagon bumped on the road. The air was cool and crisp, and leaves crunched under the wagon's tires. The tractor stopped by a large field. There were rows of pumpkins growing on tangled vines. Some were big. Some were small. Some pumpkins were orange. Some were gold.

Molly found a good pumpkin. It was long and orange. The farmer cut the pumpkin off the vine.

Comprehension Assessment: Assessment 23

1 Where do you think the story happens?

(A) at the market

(B) at school

(C) at Molly's house

(D) at a farm

2 Why is Molly there?

(F) She is picking a pumpkin at the pumpkin patch.

(G) She is eating pumpkin pie.

(H) She is helping the farmer plant seeds.

(I) She is learning to drive a tractor.

3 What season is it?

(A) spring

(B) summer

(C) fall

(D) winter

© Harcourt

Directions: Read the passage below. Fill in the circle in front of the best answer to each question.

Splash!

Jack shook his hair wildly. A spray of water sprinkled the kids around him. Kiesha counted loudly, and then she jumped in with a tremendous splash. Some kids bobbed up and down. Others splashed and kicked. It was crowded, but the water felt cool and refreshing. The sky was bright blue, and the hot sun shone brightly. Jack put on his goggles and went deep. After 45 minutes, the lifeguard blew his whistle and everyone got out.

Jack put on more sunblock. Kiesha wrapped in a thick warm towel. They sat in the shade until the break was over.

Comprehension Assessment: Assessment 24

1 Where do you think the story happens?

- Ⓐ at school
- Ⓑ at a pool
- Ⓒ at Kiesha's house
- Ⓓ at a farm

2 Why does Jack put on sunblock?

- Ⓕ There was no shade to sit in.
- Ⓖ The water was too cold.
- Ⓗ He doesn't want to get sunburned.
- Ⓘ He forgot his towel.

3 What season is it?

- Ⓐ spring
- Ⓑ summer
- Ⓒ fall
- Ⓓ winter

4 Why does everyone get out?

- Ⓕ Kiesha splashed them.
- Ⓖ They need towels.
- Ⓗ It begins to rain.
- Ⓘ It's break time at the pool.

Name _____ Date _____

Directions: Read the passage below. Fill in the circle in front of the best
answer to each question.

Pizza is the best thing you can eat. I think meat pizza is not
as good as veggie pizza. Veggie pizza often has onions and
peppers. I like how the cheese is gooey and savory. Pizza cheese is
made from milk. The perfect pizza has hot, red sauce. The sauce
is made from tomatoes. I could eat pizza for breakfast, lunch,
and dinner.

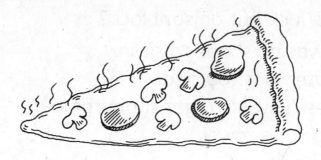

1 Which sentence is a fact?

Ⓐ Pizza is the best thing you can eat.

Ⓑ I think meat pizza is not as good as veggie pizza.

Ⓒ The perfect pizza has hot, red sauce.

Ⓓ The sauce is made from tomatoes.

2 Which sentence is an opinion?

Ⓕ I think meat pizza is not as good as veggie pizza.

Ⓖ The sauce is made from tomatoes.

Ⓗ Pizza cheese is made from milk.

Ⓘ Veggie pizza often has onions and peppers.

Comprehension Assessment: Assessment 25

Directions: Read the passage below. Fill in the circle in front of the best answer to each question.

Tony got a book of comic strips for his birthday. He thinks comic books are the best books for gifts. Everyone likes a good comic book. Comics are a form of art. Most comic strips started in newspapers. Tony thinks comics should be in color. But some newspapers print comics only in black and white. Everyone agrees that the comic strips about a boy and his tiger are the funniest comics. Comics often tell a short story. Tony does not like comics about the news.

1 Which sentence is a fact?

Ⓐ Everyone likes a good comic book.

Ⓑ Comics are a form of art.

Ⓒ Tony thinks comics should be in color.

Ⓓ Everyone agrees that the comic strips about a boy and his tiger are the funniest comics.

2 Which sentence is an opinion?

Ⓕ He thinks comic books are the best books for gifts.

Ⓖ Comics are a form of art.

Ⓗ Most comic strips started in newspapers.

Ⓘ Comics often tell a short story.

Comprehension Assessment: Assessment 25

Directions: Read the passage below. Fill in the circle in front of the best answer to each question.

Time to Wash Zip

Kara has a little dog. His name is Zip. Zip ran in mud. Now Zip needs a bath. Kara gets the towels. She finds the shampoo. She puts them by the garden hose.

"Here, Zip!" calls Kara. The dog comes to the hose.

First, Kara gets Zip wet. The water is warm. Zip looks funny with wet hair. Next, Kara puts shampoo on the dog. Then she rubs his hair. Now Zip is clean. Kara cleans off the soap. The warm water feels good. She rubs Zip dry with the towels. Finally, Zip smells good again.

© Harcourt

1 What happens first in the story?

Ⓐ Kara rubs Zip dry.

Ⓑ Zip runs in mud.

Ⓒ Kara gets Zip wet.

Ⓓ Kara cleans off the soap.

2 What happens after Kara gets Zip wet?

Ⓕ Kara puts shampoo on Zip.

Ⓖ Zip runs in mud.

Ⓗ Kara rubs Zip dry.

Ⓘ Kara finds the garden hose.

3 What finally happens at the end of the story?

Ⓐ Kara calls Zip to the garden hose.

Ⓑ Kara finds the shampoo.

Ⓒ Zip smells good again.

Ⓓ Zip gets muddy.

© Harcourt

Comprehension Assessment: Assessment 26

Name _____ Date _____

Directions: Read the passage below. Fill in the circle in front of the best answer to each question.

Rain Forest Play

Mr. Dooley's class will perform a play about the rain forest. On Monday, he passes out the scripts. Mr. Dooley assigns the parts to the students. Some kids make animal noises. Some kids are trees. Some kids are birds and other animals. After the kids get their parts, the class reads the script aloud.

The next day, the class reads the script again. Mr. Dooley gives the kids extra time to learn their parts.

On Wednesday and Thursday they work on props and costumes. They practice the play on the school stage.

Finally, on Friday, the class performs the play for the school. It is a fun way to learn about the rain forest.

Comprehension Assessment: Assessment 27

1 What happens first in the story?

ⓐ The kids perform for the school.

ⓑ They practice on the stage.

ⓒ They work on props and costumes.

ⓓ Mr. Dooley passes out the scripts.

2 What happens on Tuesday?

ⓕ Mr. Dooley gives the kids extra time to learn their parts.

ⓖ The kids get their scripts for the first time.

ⓗ They practice on the stage.

ⓘ They make costumes.

3 What finally happens at the end of the story?

ⓐ They make costumes.

ⓑ They make props.

ⓒ They practice on the stage.

ⓓ They perform the play for the school.

Name _____ Date _____

Directions: Read the passage below. Fill in the circle in front of the best
　　　　　　answer to each question.

At the Market

Grandma walks to the market. Today she buys fresh fruit.
She picks out apples and bananas. Grandma finds the flower
stand. She picks out yellow sunflowers. She likes roses, too. Then
Grandma smells warm bread. The bakery has small rolls. There is
soft bread. The market has many good things today.

Comprehension Assessment: Assessment 28

1 How can you classify apples and bananas?

   Ⓐ They are fruit.

   Ⓑ They are red.

   Ⓒ They are meats.

   Ⓓ They are breads.

2 What is <u>not</u> in the flower category?

   Ⓕ sunflower

   Ⓖ rose

   Ⓗ daisy

   Ⓘ fruit

3 What is in the bread category?

   Ⓐ apples

   Ⓑ bananas

   Ⓒ rolls

   Ⓓ sunflower

Name _____ Date _____

Directions: Read the passage below. Fill in the circle in front of the best answer to each question.

Rex wants to learn about Mickey Mouse. Rex found a book in the library. The book is about Walt Disney. The book has a table of contents.

Comprehension Assessment: Assessment 29

© Harcourt

1 Which chapter should Rex read to find out about Mickey Mouse?

(A) Chapter 2

(B) Chapter 3

(C) Chapter 4

(D) Chapter 5

2 Information about Walt Disney's movies starts on

(F) page 3.

(G) page 4.

(H) page 8.

(I) page 12.

3 What sort of information will be found in Chapter 4?

(A) Walt's movies

(B) Walt's childhood

(C) Disney amusement parks

(D) good news about Walt Disney

Directions: Read the passage below. Fill in the circle in front of the best answer to each question.

Natalie's class got a new pet hamster. The class had to vote on a name. Everyone in the class got to vote. The 20 students in Natalie's class chose between three names: Tiger, Buster, or Scooter. The teacher put the votes in a chart. The chart had columns and rows.

Hamster Vote

Name	Votes
Tiger	6
Buster	4
Scooter	10

After they voted, Natalie's teacher drew a hamster on the board. She labeled the head. She labeled the tail and feet.

© Harcourt

1 How many students voted for the name Buster?

Ⓐ 6

Ⓑ 4

Ⓒ 10

Ⓓ 20

2 What type of graphic aid did the teacher use for voting?

Ⓕ chart

Ⓖ map

Ⓗ diagram

Ⓘ graph

3 Which name got the most votes?

Ⓐ Buster

Ⓑ Scooter

Ⓒ Tiger

Ⓓ Natalie

4 What type of graphic aid with labels did the teacher make?

Ⓕ chart

Ⓖ map

Ⓗ diagram

Ⓘ graph

Comprehension Assessment: Assessment 30

Comprehension Answer Key

Assessment 1—page 1: 1 C; page 2: 1 A

Assessment 2—page 1: 1 B; page 2: 1 D

Assessment 3—1 B, 2 I, 3 A

Assessment 4—1 D, 2 F, 3 B

Assessment 5—1 B, 2 F, 3 D

Assessment 6—1 C, 2 F, 3 D

Assessment 7—1 B, 2 H, 3 A

Assessment 8—1 D, 2 H, 3 D

Assessment 9—1 A, 2 G, 3 C

Assessment 10—page 1: Row 1: second picture, Row 2: first picture, Row 3: first picture

page 2: Row 1: second picture, Row 2: second picture, Row 3: first picture

Assessment 11—page 1: 1 B, 2 F; page 2: 1 A, 2 G

Assessment 12—page 1: 1 D, 2 F; page 2: 1 B, 2 G

Assessment 13—page 1: 1 A; page 2: 1 D

Assessment 14—page 1: 1 C; page 2: 1 C

Assessment 15—1 B, 2 F, 3 C

Assessment 16—page 1: 1 C; page 2: 1 A

Assessment 17—page 1: 1 B, 2 F, 3 C; page 2: 1 B, 2 F, 3 D

Assessment 18—1 C, 2 I, 3 A

Assessment 19—1 A, 2 H, 3 C

Assessment 20—1 B, 2 G, 3 A

Assessment 21—1 A, 2 H, 3 B

Assessment 22—1 B, 2 H, 3 D

Assessment 23—1 D, 2 F, 3 C

Assessment 24—1 B, 2 H, 3 B, 4 I

Assessment 25—page 1: 1 D, 2 F; page 2: 1 B, 2 F

Assessment 26—1 B, 2 F, 3 C

Assessment 27—1 D, 2 F, 3 D

Assessment 28—1 A, 2 I, 3 C

Assessment 29—1 A, 2 I, 3 C

Assessment 30—1 B, 2 F, 3 B, 4 H

Vocabulary Contents

**Teacher Directions: Read the question and answer choices to children.
Have them fill in the circle in front of the correct answer.**

1 What would you find at a <u>feast</u>?

　Ⓐ lots of different foods

　Ⓑ many types of games

　Ⓒ a variety of animals

2 How would someone who is <u>mellow</u> feel?

　Ⓕ unkind

　Ⓖ cold

　Ⓗ relaxed

3 What happens when you <u>encourage</u> someone?

　Ⓐ You help him or her feel good about trying something.

　Ⓑ You make him or her do something silly.

　Ⓒ You take something from him or her.

4 Which of the following would you <u>prepare</u> for lunch?

　Ⓕ a car

　Ⓖ a sandwich

　Ⓗ a desk

5 How would someone who is <u>lonely</u> feel?

　Ⓐ glad

　Ⓑ sad

　Ⓒ happy

6 What happens when you <u>remind</u> someone to do something?

　Ⓕ You do something for him or her.

　Ⓖ You give him or her something.

　Ⓗ You help him or her remember.

7 What happens when you walk in <u>reverse</u>?

Ⓐ You walk forward.

Ⓑ You stop.

Ⓒ You walk backward.

8 How would someone who <u>complained</u> feel?

Ⓕ happy

Ⓖ unhappy

Ⓗ joyful

9 Which of these is <u>automatic</u>?

Ⓐ a car that moves by itself

Ⓑ a big box of blocks

Ⓒ a train that you push to make move

10 What happens when you are <u>preoccupied</u>?

Ⓕ You are playing on the playground.

Ⓖ You are busy working on your homework.

Ⓗ You are always thinking of something else.

11 How does a dog <u>differ</u> from a cat?

Ⓐ They both have four legs.

Ⓑ They make different sounds.

Ⓒ They are both animals.

12 How would someone who is <u>confident</u> feel?

Ⓕ shy

Ⓖ unsure

Ⓗ very sure

Name _____ Date _____

Directions: Fill in the circle in front of the correct answer.

1 How do you feel when you have an <u>appetite</u>?
- (A) tired
- (B) hungry
- (C) glad

2 Which of these would you like to <u>savor</u>?
- (F) a day at the park
- (G) a meal you do not like
- (H) a day cleaning your room

3 Which of these would most likely be a <u>tradition</u>?
- (A) a trip to the grocery store
- (B) a yearly family reunion
- (C) a day at school

4 What happens when you <u>proceed</u> with something?
- (F) you laugh
- (G) you stop
- (H) you continue

5 What does a person who is <u>sly</u> do?
- (A) runs with you
- (B) helps you
- (C) tricks you

6 Which of these is <u>apparel</u>?
- (F) shoes
- (G) pillows
- (H) scissors

Vocabulary Assessment 2

Directions: Fill in the circle in front of the correct answer.

7 Which of these would most likely have an <u>aroma</u>?

Ⓐ a flower
Ⓑ a chair
Ⓒ a book

8 Which of these animals is <u>gigantic</u>?

Ⓕ a duck
Ⓖ an elephant
Ⓗ a squirrel

9 What happens when you go on a <u>voyage</u>?

Ⓐ You go to a faraway place.
Ⓑ You go on a picnic at the park.
Ⓒ You go home after school.

10 How do you feel if you are <u>glum</u>?

Ⓕ pleased
Ⓖ cheerful
Ⓗ sad

11 What does a <u>whimper</u> sound like?

Ⓐ a loud, shouting sound
Ⓑ a quiet, crying sound
Ⓒ a noisy, laughing sound

12 Which of these is <u>imaginary</u>?

Ⓕ a talking pig
Ⓖ a flying bird
Ⓗ a running horse

Name _____ Date _____

Directions: Fill in the circle in front of the correct answer.

1 What happens when people <u>squabble</u>?

Ⓐ They read.

Ⓑ They argue.

Ⓒ They eat.

---

2 How would someone who makes an <u>uproar</u> feel?

Ⓕ thankful

Ⓖ joyful

Ⓗ upset

---

3 Which of these might your mom ask you to <u>tend</u>?

Ⓐ your little sister

Ⓑ her closet

Ⓒ the refrigerator

---

4 Which of these would get <u>soggy</u> if you walked through a huge puddle?

Ⓕ your hat and scarf

Ⓖ your hands

Ⓗ your socks and shoes

---

5 If someone <u>moans</u>, what does it sound like?

Ⓐ a loud scream

Ⓑ a long, low sound

Ⓒ a high pitch yell

---

6 Which of these is probably <u>scrumptious</u>?

Ⓕ a car

Ⓖ a cookie

Ⓗ a candle

Directions: Fill in the circle in front of the correct answer.

7 What is an <u>idle</u> person doing?

Ⓐ nothing

Ⓑ running

Ⓒ driving

8 How would a color that is <u>fading</u> look?

Ⓕ bolder

Ⓖ darker

Ⓗ lighter

9 What does it mean if your mom says, "<u>Perhaps</u> I will take you to the park"?

Ⓐ She will definitely take you to the park.

Ⓑ She will not take you to the park.

Ⓒ She may or may not take you to the park.

10 If you <u>prefer</u> apples over bananas or grapes, which is your favorite fruit?

Ⓕ grapes

Ⓖ apples

Ⓗ bananas

11 Which toy is likely to <u>whirl</u>?

Ⓐ a spinning top

Ⓑ a piggy bank

Ⓒ a stuffed animal

12 Which of these is your <u>property</u>?

Ⓕ your friend's jacket

Ⓖ your backpack

Ⓗ your sister's book

4

Directions: Fill in the circle in front of the correct answer.

1 Which of these most likely <u>creeps</u>?

Ⓐ a bird
Ⓑ a fish
Ⓒ a worm

2 What do you do when you <u>nestle</u> next to something?

Ⓕ snuggle
Ⓖ run
Ⓗ talk

3 How would you feel if you felt <u>delight</u>?

Ⓐ happy
Ⓑ busy
Ⓒ sorry

4 What happens outside when it is <u>blustery</u>?

Ⓕ It is raining.
Ⓖ It is windy.
Ⓗ It is calm.

5 What happens when you <u>load</u> your school bag with books?

Ⓐ You are taking books out.
Ⓑ You are giving books away.
Ⓒ You are putting books in.

6 Which of these would give you a <u>thrill</u>?

Ⓕ taking a walk
Ⓖ riding a roller coaster
Ⓗ cleaning your room

© Harcourt

Vocabulary Assessment 4

Directions: Fill in the circle in front of the correct answer.

7 How do you feel if you are <u>joyous</u>?

Ⓐ very happy

Ⓑ very mad

Ⓒ very proud

8 Which of these is a <u>fantasy</u>?

Ⓕ riding a bike to school

Ⓖ learning to play the piano

Ⓗ teaching your dinosaur tricks

9 If you <u>contribute</u> to the class project, what do you do?

Ⓐ You give something to the project.

Ⓑ You will not work on the project.

Ⓒ You do the entire project yourself.

10 What are you doing if you are <u>slumbering</u>?

Ⓕ playing

Ⓖ sleeping

Ⓗ talking

11 If you do something <u>spontaneously</u>, how do you do it?

Ⓐ You plan it very carefully.

Ⓑ You do it right away without planning.

Ⓒ You do it all wrong.

12 Which of these items is the most <u>versatile</u>?

Ⓕ a scissors

Ⓖ a shirt

Ⓗ a piece of paper

Name _____ Date _____

Directions: Fill in the circle in front of the correct answer.

1 If you <u>meander</u>, what are you doing?

Ⓐ walking very slowly

Ⓑ taking a nap

Ⓒ running very quickly

2 What do you do when you <u>tidy</u> your room?

Ⓕ You paint it.

Ⓖ You make a mess.

Ⓗ You make it neat.

3 How would someone who is <u>famished</u> feel?

Ⓐ very hungry

Ⓑ very hurt

Ⓒ very busy

4 What happens when you <u>modify</u> something?

Ⓕ You make it totally different.

Ⓖ You change it a little.

Ⓗ You give it away.

5 Which of these would most likely be <u>unfortunate</u>?

Ⓐ finding a shiny penny

Ⓑ reading a good book

Ⓒ tripping over a rock

6 Which of these is <u>sturdy</u>?

Ⓕ a pencil

Ⓖ a desk

Ⓗ an envelope

Directions: Fill in the circle in front of the correct answer.

7 Which of these would most likely be a <u>treasure</u>?

Ⓐ an old pair of socks

Ⓑ a special photograph

Ⓒ an empty water bottle

8 If you give someone a <u>compliment</u>, what have you done?

Ⓕ You said you liked something about them.

Ⓖ You played at the park with them.

Ⓗ You gave them your favorite toy.

9 What happens when people <u>confer</u>?

Ⓐ They ignore each other.

Ⓑ They sing a song.

Ⓒ They talk with others.

10 If a doll is <u>exquisite</u>, what is it like?

Ⓕ normal and ordinary

Ⓖ very special and beautiful

Ⓗ very large in size

11 What do you do when you are <u>protecting</u> something?

Ⓐ You are giving it away.

Ⓑ You are feeding it.

Ⓒ You are keeping it safe.

12 How do you feel about something you <u>adore</u>?

Ⓕ You love it a lot.

Ⓖ You don't care for it.

Ⓗ You would like to throw it away.

Name _____ Date _____ **6**

Directions: Fill in the circle in front of the correct answer.

1 Which of these would most likely move with <u>grace</u>?

(A) a football player

(B) a dancer

(C) a baby learning to walk

2 How would someone who is <u>watchful</u> look after a puppy?

(F) in an unprepared way

(G) in a careful, alert way

(H) in a cold, uncaring way

3 If you <u>constantly</u> play the piano, how often do you play?

(A) all the time

(B) never

(C) once in a while

4 Which of these places is most likely <u>lush</u>?

(F) a city street

(G) an icy lake

(H) a forest

5 If you saw a <u>marvelous</u> show, how was it?

(A) wonderful

(B) terrible

(C) short

6 Which of these might have a <u>hollow</u> space?

(F) a coat

(G) a log

(H) a book

Vocabulary Assessment 6

Directions: Fill in the circle in front of the correct answer.

7 If you saw an animal <u>scurry</u>, how was it moving?

Ⓐ rapidly hopping

Ⓑ slowly with long steps

Ⓒ quickly with small steps

8 What happens when you <u>arise</u>?

Ⓕ You fall asleep quickly.

Ⓖ You get up from sitting or lying down.

Ⓗ You lie down and take a rest.

9 How would someone who is <u>ravenous</u> feel?

Ⓐ very strong

Ⓑ very happy

Ⓒ very hungry

10 Which of these is most likely <u>lively</u>?

Ⓕ a person dancing

Ⓖ a cat taking a nap

Ⓗ a bird sitting in a nest

11 What happens when people <u>quarrel</u>?

Ⓐ they argue

Ⓑ they agree

Ⓒ they smile

12 What is a <u>clever</u> person good at?

Ⓕ painting pictures

Ⓖ solving problems

Ⓗ singing songs

Directions: Fill in the circle in front of the correct answer.

1 If you <u>dare</u> a friend to do something, what do you want the friend to do?

(A) something scary

(B) something easy

(C) something boring

---

2 Which of these might be <u>gleaming</u>?

(F) a paper bag

(G) a crayon

(H) a shiny coin

---

3 If you went to a <u>splendid</u> party, how was it?

(A) long

(B) dull

(C) wonderful

---

4 What might you do <u>cautiously</u>?

(F) read a book

(G) ride a scooter

(H) watch television

---

5 What would you do at a <u>festival</u>?

(A) eat different foods

(B) fly on airplanes

(C) play computer games

---

6 Which of these would most likely be a <u>disaster</u>?

(F) a birthday party

(G) a tornado

(H) a movie

Directions: Fill in the circle in front of the correct answer.

7 Which of these would be an <u>adventure</u>?

Ⓐ a walk to your neighbor's house

Ⓑ a trip to a faraway place

Ⓒ a swim in the local pool

___

8 Which type of place would be the best to <u>explore</u>?

Ⓕ a new place where you have never been

Ⓖ a place you have been many times

Ⓗ your own room

___

9 Which of these animals is most likely <u>tame</u>?

Ⓐ a pet bird

Ⓑ a mountain lion

Ⓒ a shark

___

10 Which of these would you be <u>amazed</u> to see?

Ⓕ a dog chewing a bone

Ⓖ a dog doing a trick

Ⓗ a dog singing a song

___

11 If you <u>completely</u> eat an apple, how much did you have?

Ⓐ all of the apple

Ⓑ part of the apple

Ⓒ none of the apple

___

12 Which of these would you have to <u>jolt</u> to move?

Ⓕ a small stone

Ⓖ a feather

Ⓗ a large bench

Directions: Fill in the circle in front of the correct answer.

1 How would someone who is <u>bothered</u> feel?

Ⓐ warm

Ⓑ glad

Ⓒ upset

2 Which of these would be the longest <u>distance</u> from your classroom?

Ⓕ the hallway

Ⓖ the moon

Ⓗ the playground

3 What are you doing when you <u>form</u> something?

Ⓐ shaping it

Ⓑ eating it

Ⓒ drinking it

4 If you are <u>supportive</u> of your brother, what do you do?

Ⓕ help him believe he can do something

Ⓖ help him finish his lunch

Ⓗ tell him he cannot do something

5 How do you pay <u>attention</u>?

Ⓐ give a lot of money

Ⓑ run away quickly

Ⓒ listen or watch carefully

6 Which of these might you want to <u>escape</u> from?

Ⓕ a fun game

Ⓖ a scary movie

Ⓗ a good book

Directions: Fill in the circle in front of the correct answer.

7 How do you feel if you feel <u>fright</u>?

Ⓐ cheerful

Ⓑ afraid

Ⓒ bored

8 If something is <u>nearby</u>, where is it?

Ⓕ close

Ⓖ distant

Ⓗ far

9 What do you do if you <u>cram</u> something into a bag?

Ⓐ You take everything out of the bag.

Ⓑ You put nothing in the bag.

Ⓒ You put too much in the bag.

10 If you <u>memorize</u> something, what have you done?

Ⓕ learned it

Ⓖ eaten it

Ⓗ given it away

11 Which of these has the largest <u>capacity</u>?

Ⓐ a small cup

Ⓑ a milk carton

Ⓒ a spoon

12 How do you feel if you are <u>proud</u>?

Ⓕ You feel sorry for something you did.

Ⓖ You feel good about something you did.

Ⓗ You feel unhappy about something you did.

Directions: Fill in the circle in front of the correct answer.

1 How did your face look if you <u>pouted</u>?

Ⓐ unhappy

Ⓑ jolly

Ⓒ happy

2 If you <u>ambled</u> to the door, how did you get there?

Ⓕ ran quickly

Ⓖ crawled slowly

Ⓗ walked slowly

3 If you are trying to <u>locate</u> something, what are you doing?

Ⓐ trying to buy something

Ⓑ trying to find something

Ⓒ trying to eat something

4 What do you do when you follow a <u>routine</u>?

Ⓕ You do something different and unusual.

Ⓖ You do not do anything.

Ⓗ You do the same thing every time.

5 Which of these would be <u>unexpected</u>?

Ⓐ a surprise birthday party

Ⓑ a scheduled appointment

Ⓒ a regular school day

6 If something is <u>horrible</u>, what is it like?

Ⓕ very good

Ⓖ very bad

Ⓗ very pretty

© Harcourt

Directions: Fill in the circle in front of the correct answer.

7 How does a person who is <u>invigorated</u> feel?

Ⓐ very silly

Ⓑ kind of sleepy

Ⓒ full of energy

8 What does a person who is <u>persistent</u> do?

Ⓕ gives up

Ⓖ keeps trying

Ⓗ gets tired

9 What does it feel like outside if it is <u>sweltering</u>?

Ⓐ very hot

Ⓑ a little cool

Ⓒ extremely cold

10 Which of these would cause a <u>commotion</u>?

Ⓕ a child yelling and screaming

Ⓖ a child riding a bike

Ⓗ a child taking a nap

11 What might be <u>overflowing</u> from a bathtub?

Ⓐ fish

Ⓑ cookies

Ⓒ water

12 What are you doing when you <u>search</u> for something?

Ⓕ You are reading something.

Ⓖ You are looking for something.

Ⓗ You are making something.

© Harcourt

Directions: Fill in the circle in front of the correct answer.

1 How do you know a flower has an <u>odor</u>?

Ⓐ You can see it.

Ⓑ You can smell it.

Ⓒ You can hear it.

2 How many people are in a <u>chorus</u>?

Ⓕ none

Ⓖ only one

Ⓗ more than one

3 If you <u>shoved</u> a chair, what did you do?

Ⓐ You pushed against it.

Ⓑ You sat down on it.

Ⓒ You stood beside it.

4 If you are <u>enthusiastic</u> about something, how do you act?

Ⓕ excited

Ⓖ sleepy

Ⓗ uninterested

5 What is left if you <u>consume</u> your sandwich?

Ⓐ all of it

Ⓑ only the bread

Ⓒ nothing

6 If you <u>gather</u> some toys, what are you doing?

Ⓕ getting rid of them

Ⓖ bringing them together

Ⓗ pushing them away

Directions: Fill in the circle in front of the correct answer.

7 What are you doing if you are <u>chatty</u>?

Ⓐ talking a lot
Ⓑ smiling a lot
Ⓒ waving both hands

8 What do people do when they <u>dine</u>?

Ⓕ run
Ⓖ sleep
Ⓗ eat

9 How would someone who <u>groaned</u> feel?

Ⓐ unhappy
Ⓑ disappointed
Ⓒ lucky

10 What is the <u>function</u> of a pair of glasses?

Ⓕ to make you smile
Ⓖ to help you see
Ⓗ to color a picture

11 Which of these foods is the most <u>nutritious</u>?

Ⓐ a cookie
Ⓑ an ice cream cone
Ⓒ a banana

12 Which of these would be a <u>duty</u>?

Ⓕ playing at the park
Ⓖ taking out the trash
Ⓗ having fun at school

Name _____ Date _____ **11**

Directions: Fill in the circle in front of the correct answer.

1 What happens when you are <u>ashamed</u>?

Ⓐ You feel like you are going to have a fun day.

Ⓑ You feel like you have done something wrong.

Ⓒ You feel like you want to rest.

2 Which of these animals has <u>soared</u>?

Ⓕ a bird

Ⓖ a cow

Ⓗ a horse

3 What is someone who is <u>athletic</u> good at?

Ⓐ cooking

Ⓑ sports

Ⓒ helping

4 How would someone who is <u>awkward</u> move?

Ⓕ in a smooth way

Ⓖ in a quick way

Ⓗ in a clumsy way

5 How does a meal that is <u>superb</u> taste?

Ⓐ terrible

Ⓑ ordinary

Ⓒ excellent

6 If an animal <u>nuzzled</u> you, what did it do?

Ⓕ rubbed against you with its face

Ⓖ shoved you with its body

Ⓗ kicked you with its leg

Vocabulary Assessment 11

Directions: Fill in the circle in front of the correct answer.

7 What happens when a fire is <u>raging</u>?

Ⓐ It has been put out.

Ⓑ It is weak.

Ⓒ It is strong.

8 Which of these is a place that people may <u>inhabit</u>?

Ⓕ the ocean floor

Ⓖ an apartment

Ⓗ the moon

9 What do you think of something that is <u>intriguing</u>?

Ⓐ You are curious about it.

Ⓑ You do not think anything about it.

Ⓒ You do not want to ever see it again.

10 How do you feel if someone is <u>cruel</u> to you?

Ⓕ bad

Ⓖ sleepy

Ⓗ good

11 How would someone who is <u>greedy</u> act?

Ⓐ He or she would give away everything.

Ⓑ He or she would not share anything.

Ⓒ He or she would be fun to be around.

12 What might be the <u>consequences</u> of not completing your chores?

Ⓕ You may not get to play outside.

Ⓖ You may get a nice snack before dinner.

Ⓗ Your mom may be very happy with you.

Directions: Fill in the circle in front of the correct answer.

1 What happens when you <u>doubt</u> something?

Ⓐ You agree with it.

Ⓑ You take it home.

Ⓒ You do not believe it.

2 What happens when you <u>continue</u> playing a game?

Ⓕ You keep playing the game.

Ⓖ You put the game away.

Ⓗ You lose the game.

3 Who might be the best person to <u>examine</u> you if you do not feel well?

Ⓐ a doctor

Ⓑ a sales person

Ⓒ a singer

4 Which of these would someone most likely <u>devour</u>?

Ⓕ a pad of paper

Ⓖ a sandwich

Ⓗ a lunch box

5 What happens when you <u>transform</u> something?

Ⓐ It disappears.

Ⓑ It totally changes.

Ⓒ It stays the same.

6 Which of these animals moves at a fast <u>pace</u>?

Ⓕ a snail

Ⓖ a turtle

Ⓗ a horse

Name —————————————— Date ——————————— **12**

Directions: Fill in the circle in front of the correct answer.

7 What might someone who is <u>energetic</u> do?

Ⓐ take a long bike ride
Ⓑ take a short nap
Ⓒ read a long book

8 If you <u>approached</u> a friend, what did you do?

Ⓕ walked away from the friend
Ⓖ moved toward the friend
Ⓗ took something from the friend

9 What happens when you <u>excel</u> at something?

Ⓐ You are very good at it.
Ⓑ You do not want to do it.
Ⓒ You are not good at it.

10 How would someone who is <u>cozily</u> lying in bed feel?

Ⓕ hot and uncomfortable
Ⓖ cold and tired
Ⓗ warm and comfortable

11 What have you done if you made an <u>accomplishment</u>?

Ⓐ You made a bad mistake.
Ⓑ You worked hard to get something done.
Ⓒ You gave up too soon.

12 What do you do if you <u>reassure</u> your sister?

Ⓕ help her finish what she is doing
Ⓖ make her give up what she is doing
Ⓗ tell her everything will be all right

© Harcourt

Vocabulary Assessment 12

169

Directions: Fill in the circle in front of the correct answer.

1 What happens when you are <u>struggling</u>?

Ⓐ You are making a great effort to do something.

Ⓑ You are doing something very easily.

Ⓒ You are walking very slowly.

2 If you have <u>captured</u> a snake, what have you done?

Ⓕ let it go

Ⓖ caught it

Ⓗ run past it

3 What is a person who is <u>amiable</u> like?

Ⓐ friendly

Ⓑ mean

Ⓒ hostile

4 Which of these events would be <u>unthinkable</u>?

Ⓕ watching a cat play with a dog

Ⓖ watching a cat climb a tree

Ⓗ watching a cat bake a cake

5 What happens when people are in <u>agreement</u>?

Ⓐ They all want to leave.

Ⓑ They all think differently.

Ⓒ They all think alike.

6 What happens if you go <u>unnoticed</u> at a party?

Ⓕ No one sees you.

Ⓖ Everyone wants to talk to you.

Ⓗ You are seen by everyone.

Directions: Fill in the circle in front of the correct answer.

7 How do you feel if you want to <u>rejoice</u>?

Ⓐ very worried

Ⓑ very happy

Ⓒ very stubborn

_____

8 If you see something <u>extraordinary</u>, what have you seen?

Ⓕ something remarkable

Ⓖ something ordinary

Ⓗ something red in color

_____

9 What happens when people <u>argue</u>?

Ⓐ They disagree silently.

Ⓑ They agree quietly.

Ⓒ They disagree loudly.

_____

10 How do you feel and act if you are <u>wary</u> of something?

Ⓕ wild

Ⓖ careless

Ⓗ cautious

_____

11 What do you do when you give a dog a <u>command</u>?

Ⓐ You put a collar on it.

Ⓑ You tell it what to do.

Ⓒ You give it some water.

_____

12 How do people who are <u>compatible</u> get along?

Ⓕ They get along very well.

Ⓖ They do not get along at all.

Ⓗ They get along only sometimes.

Vocabulary Assessment 13

Name _____ Date _____ **14**

Directions: Fill in the circle in front of the correct answer.

1 If you are speaking <u>rapidly</u>, what are you doing?

Ⓐ talking very fast

Ⓑ not talking at all

Ⓒ talking very slow

2 How would someone who is <u>courteous</u> act?

Ⓕ polite

Ⓖ rude

Ⓗ mean

3 What might a <u>devious</u> person try to do?

Ⓐ talk to you

Ⓑ help you

Ⓒ trick you

4 If you do something <u>hastily</u>, how are you doing it?

Ⓕ in a slow manner

Ⓖ in a big hurry

Ⓗ in a cheerful way

5 How would someone who is <u>grumbling</u> feel?

Ⓐ happy

Ⓑ unhappy

Ⓒ pleased

6 Which of these is a <u>dwelling</u> for people?

Ⓕ a bicycle

Ⓖ a picture

Ⓗ a house

Directions: Fill in the circle in front of the correct answer.

7 Which of these would most likely be <u>bitterly</u> cold?

Ⓐ an oven

Ⓑ a freezer

Ⓒ a refrigerator

8 Which of these would you do for <u>amusement</u>?

Ⓕ eat a snack

Ⓖ clean your room

Ⓗ go to a movie

9 How would you act if you were <u>devoted</u> to your pet?

Ⓐ You would take good care of it.

Ⓑ You would not play with it.

Ⓒ You would give it to a friend.

10 How do you show <u>sympathy</u>?

Ⓕ by jumping up and down and clapping

Ⓖ by letting others know you feel bad

Ⓗ by smiling and shaking your head

11 How do you feel if you are <u>overjoyed</u>?

Ⓐ very happy

Ⓑ very sad

Ⓒ very busy

12 How do you feel if you are <u>alarmed</u>?

Ⓕ hungry

Ⓖ relieved

Ⓗ scared

Name _____ Date _____

Directions: Fill in the circle in front of the correct answer.

1 What falls during a <u>downpour</u>?

Ⓐ rocks

Ⓑ animals

Ⓒ rain

2 If you are <u>indecisive</u>, what do you have a hard time doing?

Ⓕ making up your mind

Ⓖ walking quickly

Ⓗ eating all your food

3 Which of these would you <u>seek</u>?

Ⓐ the hat on your head

Ⓑ a lost toy

Ⓒ your feet

4 What happens when you are <u>offended</u>?

Ⓕ Your feelings are hurt.

Ⓖ You are very cold.

Ⓗ Your eyes are tired.

5 How does a person who is <u>congenial</u> act?

Ⓐ exhausted

Ⓑ nasty

Ⓒ friendly

6 How would the face of a <u>cheerful</u> person look?

Ⓕ angry

Ⓖ smiling

Ⓗ sad

Vocabulary Assessment 15

Directions: Fill in the circle in front of the correct answer.

7 What happens when people <u>congregate</u>?

Ⓐ They gather.

Ⓑ They separate.

Ⓒ They sleep.

---

8 What did a person who <u>stammered</u> have trouble with?

Ⓕ eating

Ⓖ speaking

Ⓗ running

---

9 How would someone who is <u>pleased</u> feel?

Ⓐ calm

Ⓑ happy

Ⓒ hurt

---

10 What did you do if you <u>retorted</u> to a friend's question?

Ⓕ You replied in an angry way.

Ⓖ You answered nicely.

Ⓗ You ignored it.

---

11 What does a person who is <u>unrelenting</u> never do?

Ⓐ run away

Ⓑ sleep

Ⓒ give up

---

12 Which of these would most likely be <u>puzzling</u>?

Ⓕ a magic trick

Ⓖ a magazine

Ⓗ a toy truck

Vocabulary Assessment 15

Name _____ Date _____

Directions: Fill in the circle in front of the correct answer.

1 What do people <u>usually</u> do when they get up in the morning?

(A) go to bed
(B) eat breakfast
(C) take a nap

2 How does a <u>peaceful</u> river look?

(F) calm and quiet
(G) rough and wild
(H) cold and choppy

3 If you have a <u>variety</u> of crayons, what do you have?

(A) You have many different crayons.
(B) You have only red crayons.
(C) You do not have any crayons at all.

4 What do you do on a <u>typical</u> school day?

(F) rake leaves
(G) train animals
(H) read books

5 What is a place that is <u>shadowy</u> like?

(A) bright
(B) shady
(C) sunny

6 Which of these is a <u>pale</u> color?

(F) deep purple
(G) dark red
(H) light yellow

Vocabulary Assessment 16

Directions: Fill in the circle in front of the correct answer.

7 Which of these animals is <u>similar</u> to a dog?

Ⓐ a giraffe

Ⓑ a whale

Ⓒ a wolf

8 What does a person who is <u>affectionate</u> do?

Ⓕ enjoys riding bikes

Ⓖ shows their love

Ⓗ draws beautiful pictures

9 How would someone who <u>wailed</u> feel?

Ⓐ satisfied

Ⓑ busy

Ⓒ upset

10 What happened when people <u>scattered</u>?

Ⓕ They went off in different directions.

Ⓖ They all went to the same place.

Ⓗ They went to eat dinner.

11 How do you feel if you are <u>elated</u>?

Ⓐ very sad

Ⓑ very excited

Ⓒ very annoyed

12 How do you feel if you are <u>lonesome</u>?

Ⓕ lonely

Ⓖ cheerful

Ⓗ strong

Directions: Fill in the circle in front of the correct answer.

1 How is something done <u>properly</u>?

Ⓐ backwards

Ⓑ the wrong way

Ⓒ the right way

2 If you have <u>arrived</u> at the park, what have you done?

Ⓕ You have come to the park.

Ⓖ You have left the park.

Ⓗ You have been at the park all day.

3 If you have <u>numerous</u> trading cards, how many do you have?

Ⓐ a few

Ⓑ one

Ⓒ many

4 Which of these colors is <u>vibrant</u>?

Ⓕ white

Ⓖ orange

Ⓗ brown

5 What is something you would <u>anticipate</u>?

Ⓐ a visit from your best friend

Ⓑ a trip to the doctor

Ⓒ a day spent cleaning your room

6 Which of these would be <u>prickly</u>?

Ⓕ a rock

Ⓖ a feather

Ⓗ a porcupine

Directions: Fill in the circle in front of the correct answer.

7 What happens when you <u>construct</u> something?

Ⓐ You put something away.

Ⓑ You make or build something.

Ⓒ You paint a picture.

8 What do you do when you <u>assist</u> someone?

Ⓕ You help him or her.

Ⓖ You shove him or her.

Ⓗ You walk with him or her.

9 How do you feel if you are watching something <u>tiresome</u>?

Ⓐ angry

Ⓑ excited

Ⓒ bored

10 What would a <u>tremendous</u> dog look like?

Ⓕ very small

Ⓖ very large

Ⓗ very hairy

11 What is a <u>patient</u> person like?

Ⓐ always in a hurry

Ⓑ does not complain

Ⓒ not friendly

12 How would someone who is <u>exhausted</u> feel?

Ⓕ very tired

Ⓖ very happy

Ⓗ very anxious

Vocabulary Answer Key

Assessment 1
1 A, 2 H, 3 A, 4 G, 5 B, 6 H, 7 C, 8 G, 9 A, 10 H, 11 B, 12 H

Assessment 2
1 B, 2 F, 3 B, 4 H, 5 C, 6 F, 7 A, 8 G, 9 A, 10 H, 11 B, 12 F

Assessment 3
1 B, 2 H, 3 A, 4 H, 5 B, 6 G, 7 A, 8 H, 9 C, 10 G, 11 A, 12 G

Assessment 4
1 C, 2 F, 3 A, 4 G, 5 C, 6 G, 7 A, 8 H, 9 A, 10 G, 11 B, 12 H

Assessment 5
1 A, 2 H, 3 A, 4 G, 5 C, 6 G, 7 B, 8 F, 9 C, 10 G, 11 C, 12 F

Assessment 6
1 B, 2 G, 3 A, 4 H, 5 A, 6 G, 7 C, 8 G, 9 C, 10 F, 11 A, 12 G

Assessment 7
1 A, 2 H, 3 C, 4 G, 5 A, 6 G, 7 B, 8 F, 9 A, 10 H, 11 A, 12 H

Assessment 8
1 C, 2 G, 3 A, 4 F, 5 C, 6 G, 7 B, 8 F, 9 C, 10 F, 11 B, 12 G

Assessment 9
1 A, 2 H, 3 B, 4 H, 5 A, 6 G, 7 C, 8 G, 9 A, 10 F, 11 C, 12 G

Assessment 10
1 B, 2 H, 3 A, 4 F, 5 C, 6 G, 7 A, 8 H, 9 A, 10 G, 11 C, 12 G

Assessment 11
1 B, 2 F, 3 B, 4 H, 5 C, 6 F, 7 C, 8 G, 9 A, 10 F, 11 B, 12 F

Assessment 12
1 C, 2 F, 3 A, 4 G, 5 B, 6 H, 7 A, 8 G, 9 A, 10 H, 11 B, 12 H

Assessment 13
1 A, 2 G, 3 A, 4 H, 5 C, 6 F, 7 B, 8 F, 9 C, 10 H, 11 B, 12 F

Assessment 14
1 A, 2 F, 3 C, 4 G, 5 B, 6 H, 7 B, 8 H, 9 A, 10 G, 11 A, 12 H

Assessment 15
1 C, 2 F, 3 B, 4 F, 5 C, 6 G, 7 A, 8 G, 9 B, 10 F, 11 C, 12 F

Assessment 16
1 B, 2 F, 3 A, 4 H, 5 B, 6 H, 7 C, 8 G, 9 C, 10 F, 11 B, 12 F

Assessment 17
1 C, 2 F, 3 C, 4 G, 5 A, 6 H, 7 B, 8 F, 9 C, 10 G, 11 B, 12 F

Progress Chart — Comprehension

Name_____ Teacher_____

Assessment	Score	Date Given	Comments
1 Characters	__/2		
2 Characters and Setting	__/2		
3 Setting	__/3		
4 Setting	__/3		
5 Beginning, Middle, End	__/3		
6 Plot	__/3		
7 Plot	__/3		
8 Make Predictions	__/3		
9 Make Predictions	__/3		
10 Real and Make-Believe	__/6		
11 Fiction and Nonfiction	__/4		
12 Author's Purpose	__/4		
13 Author's Purpose	__/2		
14 Author's Purpose	__/2		
15 Details	__/3		
16 Main Idea	__/2		
17 Main Idea and Details	__/6		
18 Cause and Effect	__/3		
19 Cause and Effect	__/3		
20 Compare and Contrast	__/3		
21 Compare and Contrast	__/3		
22 Draw Conclusions	__/3		
23 Make Inferences	__/3		
24 Make Inferences	__/4		
25 Fact and Opinion	__/4		
26 Sequence	__/3		
27 Sequence	__/3		
28 Classify/Categorize	__/3		
29 Locate Information	__/3		
30 Use Graphic Aids	__/4		

Progress Chart — Vocabulary

Name_____ **Teacher**_____

Assessment	Score	Date Given	Comments
Assessment 1	__/12		
Assessment 2	__/12		
Assessment 3	__/12		
Assessment 4	__/12		
Assessment 5	__/12		
Assessment 6	__/12		
Assessment 7	__/12		
Assessment 8	__/12		
Assessment 9	__/12		
Assessment 10	__/12		
Assessment 11	__/12		
Assessment 12	__/12		
Assessment 13	__/12		
Assessment 14	__/12		
Assessment 15	__/12		
Assessment 16	__/12		
Assessment 17	__/12		